Venice

APA PUBLICATIONS
Part of the Langenscheidt Publishing Group

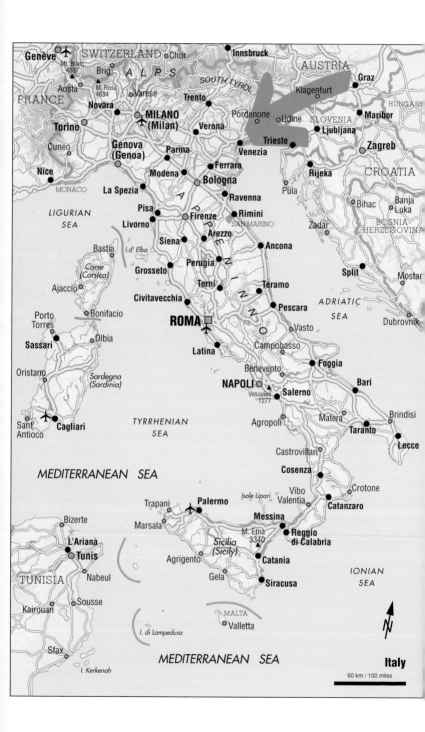

Italy

60 km / 100 miles

Welcome

This guidebook combines the interests and enthusiasms of two of the world's best-known information providers: Insight Guides, who have set the standard for visual travel guides since 1970, and Discovery Channel, the world's premier source of non-fiction television programming. Its aim is to help visitors get the most of Venice, a place which is more a stage-set than a city and apt to overwhelm and confuse as well as dazzle and mesmerise.

One of Insight's experts on Venice, Susie Boulton, has therefore devised a range of itineraries to cut through this sense of disorientation. The first three tours, aimed at visitors with just three days to spend in the city, link the essential sights, and then eight further itineraries explore certain areas and aspects of the city in more detail. Supporting the itineraries are chapters on history and culture, eating out and nightlife, plus a practical information section. As well as covering the must-see museums, palaces and squares, the book also tries to show a different Venice, seemingly miles, but only minutes, from the madding crowds: quiet corners where lacemakers and gondola builders still carry on their work and where many of the most rewarding museums, churches and palazzi are found.

Susie Boulton, a writer and art historian, has been a regular visitor to Venice for some 25 years, both for pleasure and while undertaking writing and research assignments. There is nowhere, she says, to match Venice for beauty and charm. It is a city that invites exploration. In this guide her purpose is to 'show you the quintessential magic of Venice, so that when you step back into reality, where the houses are built on terra firma, it takes time and a tug to readjust.'

HISTORY AND CULTURE

From the city's heyday as the hub of the silk and spice trades to the current fight to save it from sinking into the sea – an introduction to Venice's rich and fascinating history and culture **11–17**

CITY ITINERARIES

The first three full-day itineraries link the must-see sights, such as the Piazza San Marco, the Doge's Palace, the Accademia and some of the loveliest churches in the city. A selection of shorter itineraries are intended for visitors with more time to spend in Venice, with tours 4–7 designed as morning options, and 8–11 as afternoon suggestions.

Pages 2/3: view over San Marco basilica
Pages 8/9: gondolas – a symbol of Venice

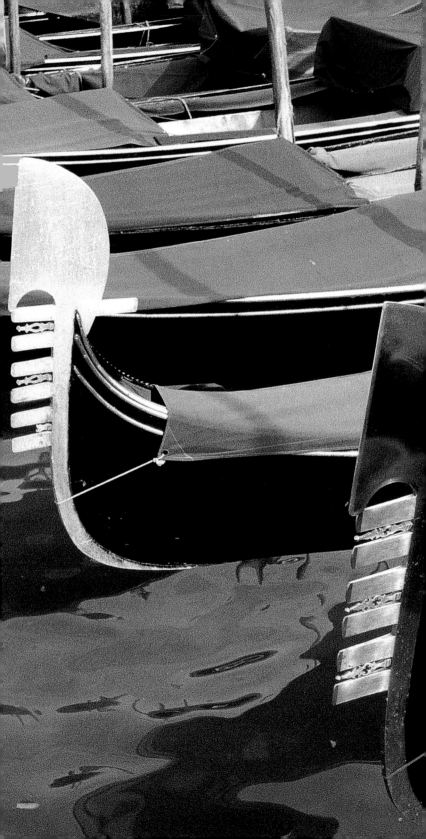

History & Culture

The mudflats and swampy marshes of the Venetian lagoon held little allure for the barbarian marauders who swept into Italy in the 5th century AD. So it was on these low-lying lagoon islands that the local inhabitants, fleeing from the onslaught, sought sanctuary. The settlers were a sociable lot and by the 7th century they had founded a kind of duchy ruled from Byzantium. By the beginning of the 9th century the seat of the settlement was the *Rivus Altus*, a group of islands named after a deep channel that divides them. These islands became known as the Rialto.

The Arab conquest of Egypt and the Levant had left the Byzantine Empire low on food supplies and it was Venetian merchants who filled the gap. The Rialto became a key trading centre where spices, silks and other luxuries from the East were exchanged for corn, salt, oil and such basic provisions from the West. This marked the beginning of Venice's vast commercial expansion and the foundation of its civilisation. Little by little, as trade expanded, Venice threw off its Byzantine yoke. By the year 1000 the Orseolo dynasty ruled in the Rialto and the independent authority of Doge Pietro Orseolo II was recognised by Constantinople. In the late 11th century, in return for their assistance in kicking the Normans out of Greece, Venetians were granted trading privileges over other merchants. Venice had truly come of age.

Alliance with the Crusaders

During the 13th century Venice became increasingly powerful as a result of its deft use of commerce and diplomacy. The most significant (though ignominious) event was the Fourth Crusade, which initially set out to attack the centre of Muslim power in the Near East, but which ultimately brought about the destruction of the Christian Byzantine Empire. In return for payment and an equal division of the conquered territories, Venice agreed to provide the transport for the crusade. As it turned out, the city decided to waive payment in return for the crusaders' help in Venice's reconquest of Zara, lost to Hungary in 1186. When Zara fell, Venice persuaded the crusaders, in the teeth of papal opposition, to divert their mission to Constantinople. In 1204, the Byzantine emperor was deposed, the city was sacked and a *de facto* government established by the Venetians and crusaders. The enormous quantity of booty transported to Venice included the famous bronze horses of San Marco.

In the 13th century Venice possessed a chain of ports and supply bases through Dalmatia to Constantinople and the Black Sea. Such coveted acquisitions inevitably attracted the envy of commercial competitors, especially Genoa, which had also been

PAX EVA
TIDI NGE
MARLISTA
CE · MEVS

Left: 17th-century Rialto
Right: the lion of San Marco

granted trading privileges by Byzantium and which was hoping to establish its own trading monopoly in the eastern Mediterranean. Such hegemony would necessarily involve the defeat of Venice, the bitter enemy. Naval battles ensued and the intense rivalry climaxed in the great war of Chioggia: the Genoese fleet entered the Venetian lagoon, captured and sank Venetian ships and blocked off escape routes. The Genoese appeared to be on the verge of victory but, under Doge Andrea Contarini, Venice built a new fleet and barricaded the canals. Turning defence into attack, it besieged and finally defeated the Genoese navy at Chioggia in 1380. The war exhausted Genoa financially and marked the beginning of that city-state's maritime decline.

Democracy Limits the Doge

By the end of the 14th century Venice had developed a true republican constitution, full of checks and balances. The position of the doge had passed from one of supreme authority to that of an elected constitutional monarch. In 1355 Doge Marin Falier had tried to hijack the growing power of Venice's governing bodies and was consequently executed for treason. As the constitution developed, so the doge's powers diminished. He was elected by an aristocratic oligarchy under a complex voting system and took a solemn oath not to attempt to exceed his powers.

By the 15th century these powers were curtailed to the extent that he was not permitted to leave Venice or speak to foreign visitors in private. The weightiest decisions of state, such as the appointment of ministers and the declaration of war, were taken by the Great Council, whose 480 members were nominated by the six *sestieri* – the official districts of Venice. The more wieldy Council of State, which grew from 60 to 300 members, made the everyday executive decisions. Smaller in size, yet of vital importance to the security of the republic, was the Council of 10. This body, a cross between a court of law and a secret intelligence service, sent traitors – such as the celebrated *condottiere*n Carmagnola – to the gallows.

The 15th century witnessed the zenith of Venetian power. At the dawn of the century, in addition to its maritime pre-eminence, Venice ruled the greater part of the Veneto region north of the city, and was moving deeper into the mainland. Under the aggressive, western-orientated policy of Doge Francesco Foscari, its dominions stretched to Brescia and Bergamo and then to Ravenna and the River Adda.

The belligerent Pope Julius II, who wanted little more than to see Venice's power reduced to that of an insignificant fishing port, formed a wide-reaching alliance with the Holy Roman Empire, Spain, France, Naples, Milan and a number of other Italian states. Venice was forced to cede many of its recent acquisitions (albeit temporarily) and, worse still, was subjected to an embarrassing public humiliation: its ambassadors were obliged to kneel before the pope while the terms of their city's submission were declaimed.

A more dangerous threat came from the east. In 1453, after many attempts, the Ottoman Turks finally took Constantinople, thereby heralding the arrival

Left: Bellini's portrait of Doge Loredan
Right: paintings by Tintoretto (top) and Canaletto

of a new power in Europe. Venice sought to maintain its commercial dominance in the east, mainly through diplomatic appeasement, but at times was left with little option but to confront the Turks. Venice lost key Greek and Albanian ports in the war of 1463–70, and the Peloponnese and parts of its Adriatic shores in 1499–1503. A third blow, at the turn of the 15th century, was Vasco da Gama's success in sailing round the Cape of Good Hope. This led to the establishment of the Portuguese spice trade and the end of Venice's virtual monopoly.

Venetian Art

Although the seeds of decline were being sown abroad, on a cultural level Venice continued to prosper. Painters such as the Bellinis, Titian, Carpaccio, Giorgione, Tintoretto and Veronese gave new impact to Renaissance art by their original use of colour and light *(see Itinerary 3, page 35)*. The patrons of art in Venice were the doge, the commercial aristocracy and the *scuole* – devotional and charitable organisations that decorated their buildings with lavish works by leading artists. Venice had become a major cultural centre and an increasing number of visitors came to see the city's artistic wonders.

While the Renaissance flourished in Florence, the distinctive Venetian Gothic aesthetic – the masterpiece being the Ca' d'Oro – was at its height. With the Renaissance came Mauro Coducci (who built the first Renaissance church in Venice), the Lombardi family, who produced some of the city's finest sculpture and churches, and Sansovino, the architect of the Library, the Mint and the Loggetta. A little later came Palladio, an exponent of strict classical form and the most influential of all Italian architects. The only

churches he built happen to be in Venice. San Giorgio Maggiore and the Redentore are unsurpassed in their cool, rational, classical beauty.

Venetian Renaissance architecture has a very distinctive feel. Palladio excepted, it is as much about the rational use of a variety of architectural traditions as the consistent application of the classical form. Another typical characteristic is the absence of fortification in its *palazzi* (palaces). Moreover, the light, reflected in the waters of the city, tends to soften shadows, dematerialise form and thereby give a joyful lightness to the buildings.

The 16th century witnessed the rise of the Habsburg dynasty which, by the middle of the century, was ruling – directly or indirectly – in the Italian city states of Milan, Naples, Sicily, Sardinia, Genoa and Florence. Venice applied a policy of watchful passivity, by which it was able to retain its independence. In the East Venice wanted to continue its strategy of appeasing the Ottoman Empire, but in 1570 the sultan demanded possession of Cyprus, an island owned, and cherished, by Venice. When the Venetians refused to comply with this aggressive demand, Nicosia was sacked and the island taken by the Turks with terrible bloodshed. The Turks' aggression prompted a historic, courageous reaction that was celebrated throughout Christendom.

The Battle of Lepanto

In 1571 a Christian fleet, including many Venetian ships, won a great victory off Lepanto with the loss of 30,000 Turks and the destruction of hundreds of Turkish galleys. Unhappily for Venice this did not mark the beginning of a sustained fight; shortly afterwards Venice sued for peace and recognised the loss of Cyprus. At home bubonic plague had reduced the population by about a third. Scarcely had Venice recovered from the effects of a further plague in 1630 when the Turkish army landed in Crete and Venice was forced to cede another important stronghold. Despite the military victories that followed, Venice was never to return to its former glory.

Above: Venice was occupied by the despised Austrians in the 19th century

history/culture

During the 18th century Venice was in terminal political and commercial decline. Venetian life became hedonistic and decadent. The ruling classes abandoned themselves to the pursuit of leisure and luxury, frittering away the fortunes they had made during the republic's heyday. Life was a perpetual round of festivals and masked balls, music and gambling. This was the era of the notorious libertine, Casanova, and the great artist Tiepolo, whose illusionistic frescoes are appropriately sensuous and carefree.

The Last Doge

In 1789 Ludovico Manin, a weak, newly arrived aristocrat from the Friuli, was appointed doge. Seven years later Napoleon's troops marched into northern Italy and took Venetian Verona. Napoleon offered the republic an alliance and, on its refusal, sent General Juno to the Rialto with an ultimatum. Some citizens called for resistance but most realised that that they were in no position to fight. The Great Council convened. The sound of a shot – believed by the councillors to have been fired by a revolutionary, but in fact fired by a friendly parting Dalmatian sailor – sent them scurrying to the ballot boxes. They voted overwhelmingly for surrender. Manin was the last doge and 1,000 years of *La Serenissima* had come to an end.

At the close of the Napoleonic wars, Venice, along with substantial parts of Italy, was subjected to the sovereignty of the almost universally hated Austrians. It did not take long for Italian patriotism to spread across the peninsula. The Venetians rose up against the Metternich government, forced the Austrians to withdraw and set up a new republic. The city was besieged; five months of hunger, disease and bombs (dropped from balloons in what was the first air raid in history) forced Venice to surrender in August 1849, and Austrian rule was reimposed. In 1861 the greater part of Italy was unified and, five years later, Venice became part of the new kingdom of Italy.

Geographically, Venice is unique. It is built on an archipelago of 118 islets, supported by billions of wooden stakes driven into the mud, and linked by 400 bridges. The only link with *terra firma* is the Ponte della Libertà. Venice is the only city in the world built entirely on water – a fact that has contributed not only to its splendour, but also to its gradual decay.

On 14 November 1966, Venice was flooded to a depth of nearly 2m (more than 6ft). A second flood followed. Under the umbrella of UNESCO, some 30 private organisations from around the world, including the USA's Save Venice Foundation, went into action to save the city. Britain's Venice in Peril Fund has been a major contributor to the restoration of monuments, and it played a leading role in the successful campaign against the plan to locate Expo 2000 in the Veneto. But, despite all the efforts, there is never enough money to insure against the problems of pollution, ecology and potential flooding. (Donations can be sent to: Venice in Peril Fund, Suite 2–3, Morley House, 314-322 Regent Street, London W1R 5AB, tel: 020 7636 6138; fax: 020 7636 6139.)

As the cost of housing and restoration rises, so

Right: Giuseppe Garibaldi, a key revolutionary figure in the unification of Italy

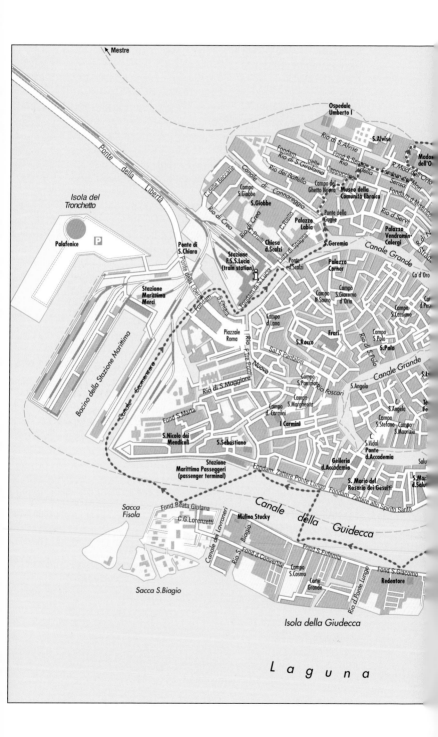

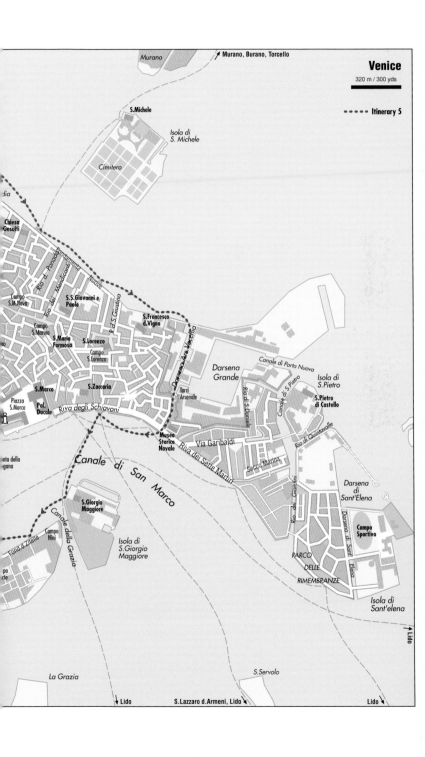

Venice

320 m / 300 yds

- - - - **Itinerary 5**

Murano

Murano, Burano, Torcello

S.Michele

Isola di
S. Michele

Cimitero

Chiesa
Gesuiti

Campo
S.M.Nova

Rio di Panada

Fondamenta
Nuove

Rio dei Mendicanti

S.S.Giovanni e
Paolo

Rio di S.Giustina

S.Francesco
d.Vigna

Campo
S.Marina

S.Maria
Formosa

S.Lorenzo

Campo
S.Lorenzo

Darsena
Vecchia

Darsena
Grande

Canale di Porta Nuova

Isola di
S.Pietro

S.Marco

Pal.
Ducale

S.Zaccaria

Piazza
S.Marco

Riva degli Schiavoni

Torri
Arsenale

Rio di S.Daniele

Canale di S.Pietro

S.Pietro
di Castello

Punta della
Dogana

Museo
Storico
Navale

Via Garibaldi

Riva dei Sette Martiri

Rio di Quintavalle

Darsena
di
Sant'Elena

Canale di San Marco

S.Giorgio
Maggiore

Campo
Nini

Canale della Grazia

Isola di
S.Giorgio
Maggiore

Secca Marina

Rio dei Giardini

Parco
Delle
Rimembranze

Darsena di Sant' Elena

Campo
Sportivo

Isola di
Sant'elena

Fond.a Zitelle

La Grazia

S.Servolo

Lido

Lido

S.Lazzaro d.Armeni, Lido

Lido

Lido

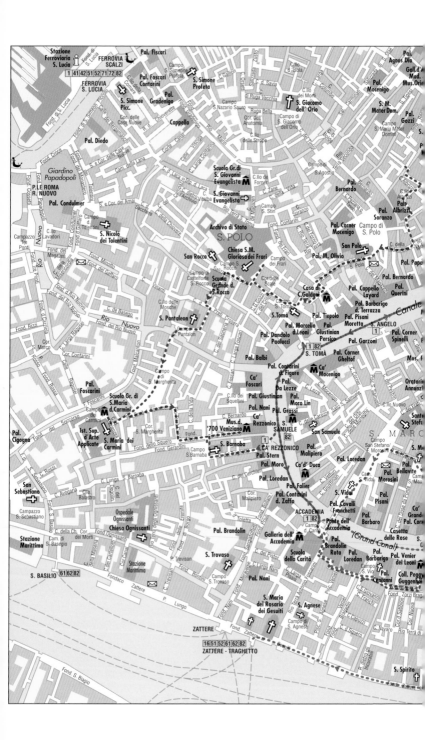

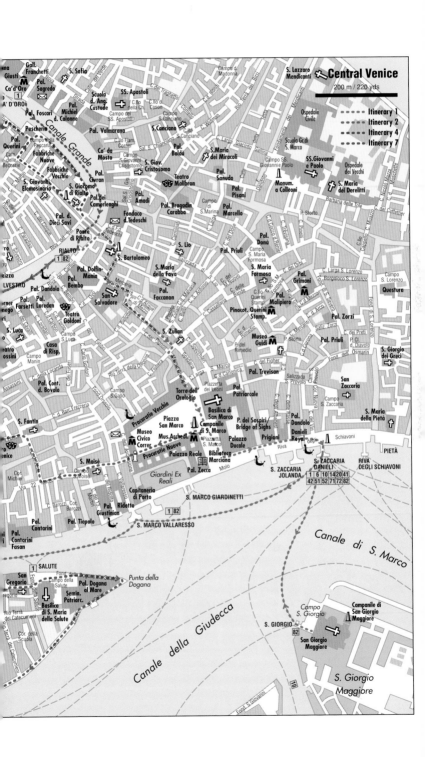

What the square – the only *piazza* in Venice – lacks in harmony is compensated by the splendour of individual architectural features. The jewel in the crown is the **Basilica di San Marco**, shrine of the Republic and symbol of Venetian glory, though it is partly shrouded in scaffolding and faux murals. The travel writer Jan Morris described the normally sumptuous exterior, which bubbles with domes and is encrusted with mosaics, marbles and carvings, as 'a barbaric building like a great Mongolian pleasure pavilion'. Mark Twain likened it to 'a vast warty bug taking a meditative walk'.

A Panorama of the City

The nearby **Campanile** (9.30–noon, 2.30–6.30pm) looks much as it did when it assumed its present form in the early 16th century. This would not be surprising were it not for the fact that it collapsed in a heap on 14 July, 1902. Amazingly, the only casualty was the custodian's cat, and Sansovino's

Loggetta at the foot of the tower, which was reassembled from the debris. A lift (daily 9am–7.30pm) operated by a monk or a volunteer from the nearby monastery will take you up to the top for a breathtaking panorama of the city and the surrounding area, stretching, on a good day, as far as the Alps. A plaque marks the water level on 4 November, 1966 – about 90cm (3ft) above ground level. The square is lined on three sides by graceful 16th- and 17th-century arcades known as the **Procuratie**, once the lavish apartments of Venice's nine procurators.

The doors of the Basilica open at 9.45am, from which time you can admire the facade at close range. Expect to see it at least partially scaffolded – viewing the building in its entirety is a rare event. The figures of four horses above the central portal are replicas of the original team looted from Constantinople during the Fourth Crusade. They were moved to the inside of the building to protect them from pollution and pigeon droppings.

Of all the mosaics decorating the entrances and upper portals, only *The Translation of the Body of the Saint to the Church of San Marco* above the door on the far left is original. Look closely to see how the basilica looked in the 13th century. The far right lower portal has a mosaic showing how the body of St Mark was taken from Alexandria, reputedly smuggled under slices of pork. Turbaned Muslims are showing their revulsion at the smell – the figure in the blue cloak is holding his nose.

For an overview of the entire basilica, the best place is the **Gallery** on the first floor. After it opens at 10am take the steep narrow steps off the narthex marked Loggia dei Cavalli to the **Marciano museum**. On this level

Above: Florian's is the prince of coffee houses. **Above Right:** the basilica interior
Right: a bird's-eye view of the Basilica di San Marco from the Campanile

you can see more easily the myriad mosaics that cover some 4,000 sq m (43,000 sq ft), and the floor, which looks like an oriental carpet. You can stand on the terrace and look down on the piazza, as doges and dignitaries did during processions and - celebrations.

On the basilica's ground level, the oldest (12th and 13th centuries) and finest of the mosaics are in the domes. The Pentecost Dome, the first as you pass through the nave, was probably the earliest to be decorated. The central dome has another spectacular mosaic, whose theme is the *Ascension of Christ*, dating from the late 12th or early 13th century.

Two Thousand Jewels

The greatest of many treasures is the **Pala d'Oro** (enter through the St Clement Chapel on the right of the rood screen; 9.45am–5.30pm, Sun 2–4.30pm) behind the altar. First commissioned for Doge Pietro Orseolo in the 9th century, and enriched over the years, it is encrusted with pearls, sapphires, emeralds and enamels. Even after Napoleon's looting, there are still about 2,000 jewels. More Byzantine loot is stored in the **Treasury** (entered from the right transept). The prize piece is the Pyx, an embossed silver-gilt casket in the shape of a Byzantine church.

There are many other splendid features in the basilica, among them the chapels, the rood screen and the baptistry. But there is little point in trying to cover all the details in one visit. If you have had enough Byzantine and Gothic splendour, you might appreciate a short jaunt across the water to

the island of **San Giorgio Maggiore**, perhaps the city's most picturesque landmark. Walk left along the waterfront until you come to the San Zaccaria landing stage opposite the Savoia & Jolanda Hotel. Wait for a No 82 *vaporetto* marked *circolare destra*. After a four-minute trip the boat drops you off below the church.

Step inside the cool, classical interior. The church has three Tintoretto paintings: *The Last Supper* and *Gathering of the Manna* on the chancel walls and, hanging in the Chapel of the Dead, *The Deposition*.

The Doge's Palace

The return trip affords fine views of the San Marco waterfront, particularly the florid Gothic facade of the **Palazzo Ducale** (Doge's Palace, daily, Mar–Sept: 9am–7pm, last admission 5.30pm; Oct–Feb 9am–5pm). The entrances are on the west side, via the **Porta della Carta** gateway, and on the waterfront. This was the home of the doges and the seat of Venetian government from the 9th century to the fall of the Republic in 1797. By the 14th century the Venetian head of state was little more than a figurehead, or 'a glorified slave of the Republic' as Petrarch put it. But as far as living quarters went, he couldn't complain. No other home could rival it and for many years this was the only building in Venice entitled to the name *palazzo*. Other grand residences had to be satisfied with the appellation *Ca'*, short for *casa* (house).

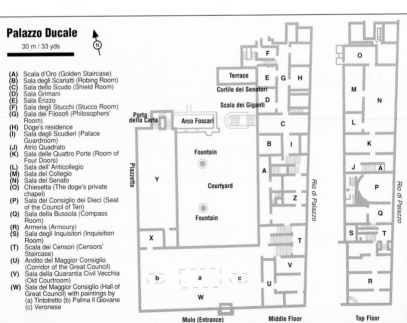

Palazzo Ducale

30 m / 33 yds

(A) Scala d'Oro (Golden Staircase)
(B) Sala degli Scarlatti (Robing Room)
(C) Sala dello Scudo (Shield Room)
(D) Sala Grimani
(E) Sala Erizzo
(F) Sala degli Stucchi (Stucco Room)
(G) Sala dei Filosofi (Philosophers' Room)
(H) Doge's residence
(I) Sala degli Scudieri (Palace Guardroom)
(J) Atrio Quadrato
(K) Sala delle Quattro Porte (Room of Four Doors)
(L) Sala dell' Anticollegio
(M) Sala del Collegio
(N) Sala del Senato
(O) Chiesetta (The doge's private chapel)
(P) Sala del Consiglio dei Dieci (Seat of the Council of Ten)
(Q) Sala della Bussola (Compass Room)
(R) Armeria (Armoury)
(S) Sala degli Inquisitori (Inquisition Room)
(T) Scala dei Censori (Censors' Staircase)
(U) Andito del Maggior Consiglio (Corridor of the Great Council)
(V) Sala della Quarantia Civil Vecchia (Old Courtroom)
(W) Sala del Maggior Consiglio (Hall of Great Council) with paintings by (a) Tintoretto (b) Palma Il Giovane (c) Veronese

Porta della Carta · Arco Foscari · Terrace · Cortile dei Senatori · Scala dei Giganti · Piazzetta · Fountain · Courtyard · Fountain · Rio di Palazzo · Molo (Entrance) · Middle Floor · Top Floor

The magnificent piece of flamboyant Gothic architecture that forms the entrance shows the Doge Foscari kneeling before the Lion of San Marco. This, together with the courtyard and Scala dei Giganti (Giants' Staircase) make an appropriately grandiose entry to the palace. Inside, the rooms are huge, with monumental canvases and heavily encrusted ceilings – all in glorification of the Venetian Republic. Few of the rooms are named and on-site information is sparse, so the official guide book is worth buying.

The gold and white stuccoed Scala d'Oro (Golden Staircase) takes you up to the doge's private apartments, then up again to the council rooms. Outstanding among these are: the **Anticollegio**, the waiting room for ambassadors, which is decorated with works by Tintoretto and Veronese's *Rape of Europe* (opposite the window wall); the **Sala del Collegio**, where the Council of State met with the doge, with its superb ceiling and some magnificent works by Veronese including *Justice and Peace Offering the Sword and Scales to Venice Enthroned*; the **Senate Room**, with another elaborate ceiling with paintings by Tintoretto and assistants; the **armoury** section; the **Sala del Consiglio dei Dieci**, where the Council of 10 (in fact about 30) tried crimes against the state, with ceiling paintings by Veronese; and – grandest of all – the **Sala del Maggior Consiglio**, the gigantic Assembly Hall, where the doges were elected and where the last doge abdicated.

The palace's proportions are monumental – some 3,000 guests were accommodated when Henry III of France was entertained here at a state banquet in 1574. The ceiling consists of panels painted by leading artists of the time, among them Tintoretto and Veronese, whose *Apotheosis of Venice* stands out for its dramatic perspective. Tintoretto's huge *Paradise*, which covers the entire east wall, was for a long time the largest painting in the world: a staggering feat for a man of 70. Below the ceiling a frieze features the first 76 doges. Note the blacked-out space that should depict Marin Falier, the doge executed for treason in 1355.

Casanova's Escape

If taking the 'secret itinerary' (for which booking is essential), you are plunged, as were the prisoners, into the dungeons. The *pozzi*, the dungeons beneath the palace, were dark, dank and infested with rats; the *piombi*, where Casanova entertained and masterminded his daring escape, were salubrious in comparison. The new prisons, which are those you see today, are reached via the **Bridge of Sighs** (where you can peep through the grills), named after the sighs of prisoners as they were led over the bridge to torture or execution – or so the story goes. In fact, by the time the bridge was built in the 17th century the cells, by European standards, were comparatively civilised and used only to house petty offenders. Only one political prisoner ever crossed the bridge.

Above Left: the view from San Giorgio Maggiore
Right: *Vecchiaia e gioventù* by Paulo Veronese on display in the Doge's Palace

It is probably now time for lunch and a rest from sightseeing. Around San Marco, whatever you choose will be expensive. For a range of prices try **Frezzeria**, west of the piazza. At the pricey end of the market, book ahead for **La Colomba**, Piscina de Frezzeria (tel: 041 522 1175; closed Wed), which is famous for fish, fashionable clientele and 20th-century paintings. Alternatively there are plenty of bars and cafés. Further west, in Ponte delle Veste, **Vino Vino** wine bar *(see Eating Out, page 73)* is good for Venetian snacks and a wide range of Italian wines.

A Vaporetto Ride

The afternoon is dedicated to a boat ride up the **Grand Canal**. Your means of travel will be the No 1 *vaporetto* which you can pick up at the San Zaccaria or San Marco landing stage. *Vaporetto* literally means little steamer, though these days they run on diesel. Despite its name, the *accelerato* No 1 is the slow boat that stops at every landing stage. Maybe buy a day ticket *(see Getting Around, page 78)* and take a boat heading in the direction of Piazzale Roma. Sit on the left side, ideally in one of the coveted prow seats.

There are more than 100 *palazzo* facades on the *Canalazzo*, as Venetians call the Grand Canal, ranging from the finely restored to the sadly dilapidated. Roughly 3.2km (2 miles) long, the canal sweeps through the heart of the city and teems with traffic of all descriptions, from gondolas to garbage barges. Guarding the canal entrance, just beyond the Customs House on the left-hand side, is the all-pervading church of **Santa Maria della Salute**, Longhena's baroque masterpiece with its huge, exuberant facade, scrolls and statues and a massive dome. At Santa Maria del Giglio (right bank), check out the delightful **Palazzo Dario**'s coloured marble, and distinctive chimneys.

Two buildings further on is the **Palazzo Venier dei Leoni**, or Palazzo Nonfinito (unfinished palace) – an incongruous two-storeyed white structure. Owners of the **Ca' Grande** on the far bank, whose view over the lagoon it would have blocked, put a stop to further building. Nonfinito now houses the **Guggenheim Collection of Modern Art** *(see Itinerary 7, page 50)*. The first

Above: take a leisurely boat trip up the Grand Canal

bridge you pass under is the wooden **Ponte dell'Accademia** (l930s). Behind the Accademia stop stands the **Scuola della Carità**, housing the Accademia gallery with the world's finest collection of Venetian paintings *(see Itinerary 2, page 31)*. Just beyond the next stop, unmistakable for its monumental stone facade, is Longhena's **Ca' Rezzonico**, arguably the finest baroque palace in Venice *(see Itinerary 7, page 50)*. Almost opposite, on the right bank, is the white stone **Palazzo Grassi**, a fine example of an 18th-century nobleman's residence, now owned by Fiat and used for major art exhibitions.

Byron and the Housekeeper

On the canal bend, just before the main tributary to the left (the Rio Foscari), stands the **Ca' Foscari**, described by Ruskin as 'the noblest example in Venice of 15th-century Gothic'. On the far side of the *rio* the **Palazzo Balbi** is an imposing late 16th-century palace. Napoleon watched a regatta in his honour here in 1807. As you stop at the San Tomà landing stage, look across to the right to the **Palazzo Mocenigo**. Byron rented this *palazzo* for £200 a year, his affair with his housekeeper ('of considerable beauty and energy… but wild as a witch and fierce as a demon') ended with the brandishing of knives and the lady flinging herself into the Grand Canal.

Just after the Sant' Angelo landing stage, look right to the **Palazzo Corner Spinelli**, a Renaissance gem designed by Mauro Coducci, distinguished by its arched windows and rusticated ground floor. Some consider it the finest Renaissance *palazzo* in Venice. Before the San Silvestro landing stage, the austere building on the right is the **Palazzo Grimani**, a Renaissance masterpiece by Michele Sanmichele that now houses the Courts of Appeal.

Disembark at the Rialto landing stage and walk up the bridge. Stroll around or choose a canalside café for a drink, then make your way back to Piazza San Marco via the **Mercerie**. Return to the Campo San Salvatore and follow the yellow signs to San Marco. Don't worry if they point in two directions – all roads eventually lead to the Piazza San Marco. The Mercerie has been a shopping thoroughfare for centuries, and today the streets are lined with lots of fabulous oriental fabrics *(see Shopping, page 61)*.

Arriving back in Piazza San Marco in the late afternoon or early evening, it is tempting to sit at an elegant café terrace to watch the evening *passeggiata*. Try **Quadri's**, which was very popular with Austrian officers during the occupation, on which grounds it is still shunned by some Venetians. The Austrians probably chose Quadri's because it was – and still is – a sun trap.

Alternatively, treat yourself to a *bellini* (champagne and peach juice) at **Harry's Bar** right behind the San Marco landing stage. Cuisine here is still regarded as among the best in Venice but it is very expensive, so when it comes to dinner you might want to try the **Al Covo** (Campiello della Pescaria, Castello 3968; tel: 041 522 3812; closed Wed, Thur). Situated on a tiny square off the Riva degli Schiavoni, this is a pricey yet stylish and civilised place specialising in Venetian fish dishes.

Right: a break by the water

2. PIAZZA, PAINTINGS AND PALACES *(see map, p20–21)*

This triangular tour travels from Piazza San Marco to two other focal points of Venice: the Accademia Gallery, which houses the world's finest collection of Venetian art, and the Dorsoduro neighbourhood, which is one of the most charming in the city.

Begin your day at Piazza San Marco to absorb a little more of this sumptuous square. Your eye will inevitably be drawn to the basilica – you might like to spend another half hour or so picking out details you missed during Itinerary No 1. Spare some time for the **Piazzetta**, the sunny square with splendid views across to the island of San Giorgio Maggiore. Here you can admire the architectural masterpieces of Sansovino who, until the arrival of Palladio, was the city's leading architect. The **Sansoviniana Library**, praised by Palladio as the richest building since antiquity, is generally acclaimed as Sansovino's masterpiece. He is also responsible for the severe **Zecca** (the Mint, beside the library and facing the lagoon) and, more in harmony with the library, the **Loggetta** at the foot of the Campanile.

Where Venetians Fear to Tread

The two massive columns in the Piazzetta, which were brought from the Orient in the 12th century, are surmounted by statues of the recently restored winged lion of S Marco and S Teodoro, who was the patron saint of Venice until the body of San Marco was brought from Alexandria. The engineer who managed to set up the columns in 1172 was rewarded with the gambling monopoly in Venice. Executions took place between the pillars, which is why superstitious Venetians don't walk between them. Leave Piazza San Marco at the western end. For a free map and list of opening times and events call in at the **tourist office** on Piazza San Marco 71 *(see page 88)*. The street

Above: the Loggetta at the foot of the Campanile
Left: city symbol

straight ahead (where you might well be distracted by shops with big designer names) will lead you into the Campo San Moisè. Contrast the overwhelming baroque detail on the church facade with the stark facade of the Bauer Grünwald Hotel, which is conspicuous as one of Venice's very few modern intrusions. Cross the bridge into the Calle Larga XXII Marzo, a broad shopping street *(see Shopping, page 62)* named after the day when the patriots reclaimed the Republic from the Austrians during the 1848 uprising.

La Fenice

Divert north along the Calle della Veste (or Calle dell Sartor da Veste), over the bridge and into the charming **Campo San Fantin**. To your right stands the late Renaissance church of San Fantin, to the left the rubble of **Teatro La Fenice**, whose solemn neoclassical facade once fronted one of the loveliest opera auditoriums in the world. In 1838 it was almost completely destroyed by fire, but it rose again 'like a phoenix' *(fenice)*, rebuilt almost exactly as it used to be. Fire struck again in 1996, forcing the opera house to move to the tented Palafenice while La Fenice is rebuilt *(for details and bookings see Calender of Events, page 75)*. To the left of the Fenice site, the house with the open-air staircase was a notorious brothel in the 16th century. Bordering the north of the square the **Ateneo Veneto** was once the headquarters of the Scuola di San Girolamo, a charitable body whose members

chaperoned criminals to the scaffold and ensured they were given a decent burial.

Take the street on the far side of the Fenice, turn left at the end under the colonnade and cross the bridge. Turn left into the little Campiello dei Caleghieri, over the bridge and along the pretty Fondamenta della Fenice, where you can see the water entrance to the opera house with its blue and yellow mooring posts. The first right turning leads you into the Campo Santa Maria del Giglio, whose church, with its baroque ornamentation and secular statuary, appalled Ruskin. Stop here to see the painting by Rubens inside the chapel.

Turn right out of the square and follow the yellow signs for the Accademia until you come to the large, rambling **Campo Santo Stefano**, otherwise known as the Campo Francesco Morosini. This was the site of the last bullfight in 1802. Stop here for coffee, preferably at **Paolin**, almost opposite the church. Paolin's ice creams are excellent. In the centre of the square is a statue of Nicolò Tommaseo, the Dalmatian scholar who, along with Daniele Manin, led Venetian resistance against the Austrian rulers in the 19th century.

As you head south from the square, cast a leftward glance to the massive **Palazzo Pisani**, a rarity in that its *campo* facade is as fine as that facing the canal. Pass the deconsecrated church of San Vidal on your right, then note the red house on the far side of the *rio* where Aldous Huxley wrote part of *Brave New World*. Stop on the Accademia bridge for splendid views of the

Above: look out for the yellow signposts

Salute. On the far side of the bridge turn right for the **Accademia Gallery**, which has the world's richest collection of Venetian painting. Spend an hour or two here using Itinerary 6 *(see pages 46–49)* as your guide.

Lunch involves a detour to the **Antica Locanda Montin** (Fondamenta di Borgo, Dorsoduro; tel: 041 522 7151; closed Tues evening and Wed), a renowned but touristy trattoria west of the gallery. Turn left as you come out, following the yellow signs for Piazzale Roma and Ferrovia. Follow the general flow across the Ponte delle Maravegie, carry straight on past bars, shops and the **Libreria alla Toletta**, which is a good bookshop. At the small bridge, by a *pasticceria*, turn left. At the canal another left turn will bring you to the restaurant. The walls of this former haunt of writers and artists are covered with paintings, some of which were bartered for meals. Sit here or in the garden under the vine for *antipasto Montin*, *malfatti alla panna* (delicious creamy pasta), grilled fish fresh from the Adriatic and tiramisù.

A Rare Public Seat

The afternoon is for leisurely strolling, browsing in boutiques or bookshops or exploring secluded corners that lie off the main thoroughfares. Begin with the eastern section of the Dorsoduro, a smart residential quarter of pretty sunlit squares, narrow canals and hidden gardens. Starting at the Accademia, work eastwards, zigzagging behind Grand Canal *palazzi*. Pause at **Campo San Vio**, sit on the red bench beside the Grand Canal (seats in the city are a rare bonus) and watch the activity on the water. Look across to the right at the massive **Ca' Grande**, whose owners, the Corner family, were said to have made their fortune through extremely dubious means. On the near side stands the **Casetta delle Rose**, where Antonio Canova had his studio in the 1770s. To your left (second from the bridge) you will see the Palazzo Barbaro, where Claude Monet and John Singer Sargent painted, Robert Browning gave readings and Henry James wrote *The Aspern Papers*.

Turn left out of the square, past the English Church, whose doors were made out of British World War I cannons, and follow the street till you come to the rear of the Palazzo Venier dei Leoni, which houses the **Guggenheim Collection of Modern Art**. You can spend an hour or so here *(see Itinerary 7, page 50)* admiring the paintings and sculpture once owned by the late Peggy Guggenheim. Carry on to **Campiello Barbaro**, a pretty square with a print shop, a frame shop, and views of the chimneys on the Palazzo Dario. Pass the Salviati glass showrooms in a grand palace setting and, further along, more glass at Cenedese, where you can watch glass-blowers at work. In the Campo San Gregorio, the deconsecrated Gothic brick church of San Gregorio is now used as a workshop for restoring paintings. Its former monastery lies to the left. The doorway of No 172 hides what Ruskin described as 'the loveliest *cortile* I know in Venice'.

Cross a tiny bridge to Longhena's domed **Basilica di Santa Maria della Salute**, erected to commemorate the deliverance of Venice from the plague of 1630. A baroque church of monumental proportions,

Left: the Punta della Dogana's golden globe

it sits atop more than a million timber piles at the entrance to the Grand Canal. After the exuberant impression of the exterior, the interior (daily 8am–noon, 3–6pm) is somewhat severe in sober grey and white. Head for the Sacristy and its works of art by Tintoretto and Titian.

Bronze Atlases

If you follow the embankment beyond the Salute you will find yourself at the **Punta della Dogana**, the 17th-century customs house. Its tower has two bronze Atlases supporting a golden globe and the charming figure of Fortuna, which together form a weather vane. From the tip of the Dorsoduro you can take in the great sights of San Marco, the island of San Giorgio Maggiore and the landmarks along Giudecca. The Guggenheim conglomerate is eyeing the disused customs houses behind you – a prime site for another gallery.

Follow the waterside to the **Zattere**, the long quayside that skirts the Giudecca Canal. From here you can look across to the island of Giudecca or the boats on the Giudecca Canal. Pass the Calcina Pensione where Ruskin stayed as an old man. If the **Gesuiti church** is open (daily 8am–noon, 5–7pm), check out the ceiling frescoed by Tiepolo.

Choose a café terrace and watch the waterbuses chugging across to Giudecca. If it is sunny, while away the early evening and eat at a waterside restaurant. The chef at the **Riviera Restaurant** (Zattere, Dorsoduro 1473, tel: 041 522 7621) trained at the far more expensive Harry's Bar. Try the homemade pastas – the *gnocchi al gorgonzola* is excellent.

Above: the red bench by the Grand Canal
Right: Basilica di Santa Maria della Salute

Quiet Corners of Castello

300 m / 330 yds

----- Itinerary 3

3. QUIET CORNERS OF CASTELLO *(see map, p34)*

A day exploring the eastern region of Venice, known as Castello. Start at the bustling waterfront close to San Marco, work your way north to the great Gothic church of Santi Giovanni e Paolo (known as San Zanipolo), passing through quiet streets and squares.

This tour covers some of the finest art and architectural treasures in the city and ends with a choice of *cicchetti* (snacks) in a Venetian wine bar or a slap-up meal in one of the best restaurants in the city.

Start the morning at the **Molo**, the busy waterfront south of the Doge's Palace, where gondolas sway by the quayside and camera-clicking crowds admire the views across the water to the shimmering island of San Giorgio Maggiore. Pick your way through stalls of souvenirs and easels of lightning sketch-artists and cross the Ponte della Paglia. Look left for the **Bridge of Sighs**. Cross a bridge to the **Riva degli Schiavoni**, a curving promenade skirting the *sestiere* of Castello, and named after the Dalmatian sailors who used to moor their trading boats and barges along the waterfront. It is still a scene of intense activity, as *vaporetti, motoscafi*, barges, tugs and cruisers moor at the landing stages and ferries chug across to the islands. On a sunny day this is a lovely spot to stop for coffee, preferably at an open-air terrace with uninterrupted views across the lagoon (but beware the prices!).

Beyond the former prisons, the luxury **Danieli Hotel** *(see Hotels, page 82)* occupies the Gothic Palazzo Dandolo and the modern aberration next door. The hotel has occupied the main building since 1822 and in that time has opened its door to many an illustrious visitor, including Wagner, Ruskin, Balzac, Proust and Dickens, who took delight in describing the horrors of the prisons next door.

Cross over the colonnaded Ponte del Vin and take the second turning to the left, under the *sottoportego* signposted to San Zaccaria. This brings you to a quiet *campo*, flanked on one side by the part-Gothic and part-Renaissance façade of the church of **San Zaccaria** (10am–noon, 4–6pm). The upper section, by leading Renaissance architect, Mauro Coducci, is particularly fine. In the 16th century the adjoining convent – not unlike other convents in the city – was notorious for its riotous, amoral nuns.

Inside the church, start with the chapels and crypt, reached by an entrance on the right-hand side. If closed apply to the custodian. The Chapel of St Athanasius, with paintings by Palma Vecchio, Titian and Tintoretto, leads to the **Capella di San Tarasio**, the former chancel, whose vault is decorated with frescoes by the Florentine master, Andrea Castagno. The crypt, usually flooded, lies below. The greatest work of art is in the main church: Giovanni Bellini's glorious *Sacra Conversazione* above the first altarpiece on the left. This is one of the finest paintings in all of

Right: the famed Bridge of Sighs

Venice – a compelling work where the serene, meditative figures are integrated by soft shadow and rich, mellow hues.

Leave the church and the square via the archway. Turn right into Campo San Provolo, go under the *sottoportico* and, just beyond a bead-shop, you will come into the **Fondamenta dell'Osmarin** (*osmarin* meaning rosemary). On a corner on the far side of the canal is the red-brick **Palazzo Priuli**, one of the finest Venetian Gothic palaces. At the end of the canal cross the two bridges and look right to the church of **San Giorgio dei Greci** with its tall, tilted bell-tower. Take the narrow alley straight ahead, pass the pretty Campiello de la Fraterna on the left and join Salizzada dei Greci. You may wish to stop off here for lunch at the **Trattoria Di Remigio**, which is excellent value. At the far end of the street cross over the bridge and turn left. Follow the canal along the Fondamenta dei Furlani and you will encounter the **Scuola di San Giorgio degli Schiavoni** (9.30am–noon, 3.30–6.30pm; closed pm Mon and Sun), founded by the Dalmatians to protect their community in Venice. The *scuola* is tiny, but is decorated with an exquisite frieze of paintings by Carpaccio illustrating the lives of the Dalmatian patron saints, St George, St Tryphon and St Jerome. The scenes are rich in colour, remarkably vivid and detailed, giving a good idea of what life was like in Venice at the turn of the 16th century.

Lost Tombs and Rambling Squares

Coming out of the Scuola, cross the bridge and turn right following the canal northwards. Just before a portico take a left turn down the Calle San Lorenzo for the church of **San Lorenzo**, which is now a hospice. Marco Polo is said to have been buried here but his tomb was lost when the church was rebuilt in 1592. Cross the bridge at the other side of the square, turn immediately right, then first left down the Borgoloco San Lorenzo. Cross the canal of San Severo, pausing on the bridge to see some fine *palazzi* on the far side, pass under the dark and narrow *sottoportego*, carry straight on, then take a right turn for the lovely **Campo di Santa Maria Formosa**. This rambling square, once the site of bullfights and open-air theatre, is full of Venetian life, its daily market stalls selling fruit and vegetables. It is flanked by *palazzi* and dominated by the swelling apses of Coducci's church of **Santa Maria Formosa**. *Formosa*, meaning both beautiful and buxom, seems appropriate.

If you are ready for lunch, pizzerias in the square provide a cheerful, open-air setting. For something more authentic try the **Al Mascaròn** *(see page 67)* on Calle Lunga Santa Maria Formosa, the narrow street to the east

Above Left: wedding in the church of San Zaccaria
Right: ceiling in the chapel of St Dominic

of the square. It is an inconspicuous old-fashioned *osteria* where you will find well-prepared snacks, excellent fish, good wines and lots of locals. Solid wooden tables and paper tablecloths are the order of the day. Save coffee until you come to the **Campo Santi Giovanni e Paolo** to the north. Take the tiny street almost opposite Al Mascaròn, cross a quiet canal and go straight on until you come to the square. Sit at one of the cafés this side to absorb the wealth of architecture and sculpture around you and imagine the splendour of the scene in the days when the square bordered the lagoon.

The Pantheon of Venice

On your right is the church of **Santi Giovanni e Paolo**, more familiarly known as San Zanipolo. This huge brick edifice vies with the Frari as the greatest Gothic church in Venice. After the tiny streets of Castello its towering, austere form makes a dramatic impact. Next to it and facing you is the rich Renaissance façade of the **Scuola Grande di San Marco**, once the meeting house of silk dealers and goldsmiths, now the civic hospital (ambulances are usually moored in the adjoining canal). Look at the *trompe l'oeil* arches framing lions that appear to be looking from the far end of deep Renaissance porticos – in fact they are barely 152mm (6 ins) deep. Close by, on a pedestal, stands what is considered one of the finest Renaissance sculptures: **the equestrian statue of Bartolomeo Colleoni,** by Verrocchio. A famous *condottiere*, Colleoni was immensely rich and offered the city of Venice a huge sum of money if it granted him an equestrian monument 'in front of San Marco'. This ran contrary to Venetian tradition but, eager to get their hands on Colleoni's fortune, the government found the answer: since the will did not stipulate the Basilica, the statue would stand in front of the Scuola San Marco instead.

The church doors of San Zanipolo reopen at 3pm. The interior of this stately Gothic structure is remarkably spacious. Known as the Pantheon of Venice, it contains the tombs of 25 doges. Identifying them is impossible without a detailed guide or the official booklet, available in the sacristy. Finest of all is Tullio Lombardo's *Monument to Doge Andrea Vendramin*

(1476–8) on the left-hand side of the apse. The figures are exquisitely grace-ful, yet at the same time natural and unaffected. To the left compare the Gothic *Monument to Doge Marco Corner*, by Nino Pisano, executed 110 years earlier. Paintings to single out are Giovanni Bellini's *St Vincent Fer-rer* polyptych located over the second altar on the right; G B Piazzetta's glowing *Apotheosis of San Dominico* on the ceiling of the San Domenico chapel (third chapel on the right); and the Veronese ceiling paintings in the Rosary Chapel.

Cross the bridge opposite the church for a brief detour to the exquisite church of **Santa Maria dei Miracoli**. Go over the next bridge and walk on to the Ponte del Povan, a lovely spot with views of three canals. Just beyond you will see the delightful geometric marble façade of the Miracoli (Mon–Sat 10am–5.30pm, Sun 1–5pm). It's a favourite place for Venetians to marry.

Return to the Campo dei Santi Giovanni e Paolo and follow the Fonda-menta dei Mendicanti (Beggars' Embankment) northwards, along the side of the hospital. You soon come to the **Fondamente Nuove** with views of the lagoon and a refreshing breeze. Turn left, cross the bridge and look across to the **island of San Michele** where the walls of the cemetery are set against a backdrop of dark leaning cypresses. Stravinsky, Ezra Pound and Diaghilev are all buried there. These are among the lucky ones that retain their graves. Most corpses are dug up after 10–12 years and taken to a public ossuary.

Baroque and Renaissance Churches

Cross the bridge beyond the last landing stage and leave the quayside by turn-ing left. This takes you past the baroque façade of the **Gesuiti church**, with stat-ues of the Twelve Apostles. It has an elaborate marble interior containing Titian's famous *Martyrdom of St Lawrence*. At this point you should follow the yellow signs for the Rialto. As you approach the bridge, spare time for a look at the Renaissance church of **San Giovanni Cristostomo**, crammed into a lit-tle square north of the Rialto. It was Mauro Coducci's last work. Inside there are

two outstanding works: Giovanni Bellini's *St Jerome with St Christopher and St Augustine*, and Sebastiano del Piombo's painting of *St John Chrysostom and Six Saints* on the high altar.

Enough sights for the day. Spend the early evening strolling down the **Rialto** and along the Riva del Carbon. At the end of this em-bankment, turn left into Calle Cavalli and look for **Al Volto** (*see Wine Bars, page 70*). This wine-tasting bar is small and popular, so ex-pect crowds to be spilling out into the street. Snacks here could fill you up for the evening, but for a more substantial meal try the **Alla Madonna**, Calle della Madonna (the other side of the Rialto; *see Restaurants, page 67*), excellent for fresh fish, or splash out at the **Ae Poste Vecie** (Tel: 041-721822), a charm-ing old trattoria behind the fish market.

Left: take an ever-popular gondola ride

4. MARKETS, MASKS AND ART *(see map, p20–21)*

Begin on the spot where the city first started: the Rialto. Browse among market stalls, then wind through the tiny alleys of San Polo to the great Gothic church of the Frari. Explore the quarter to the south and see Venetian life in some of the humbler corners of the city. End the day on the Zattere quayside, looking across the lagoon to the island of Giudecca.

For centuries the Rialto – which to most tourists is the bridge and to Venetians is the quarter around it – has been the commercial hub of the city. It was here that the first inhabitants of the lagoon are said to have settled. By the heyday of the Republic it was one of the major financial quarters of Europe – a thriving centre for bankers, brokers and merchants.

Make an early start to see the **markets** in full swing and the barges offloading at the quayside by the Grand Canal. Best days to go are Tuesday to Saturday when both main markets are functioning. Begin in the Ruga degli Orefici (signposted *Oresi*), just north of the bridge, where the market stalls create one of the most colourful scenes in Venice, with gleaming peppers and aubergines, thick sticks of asparagus, yellow-flowered *zucchini*, bags of lemons and bunches of fragrant coriander. With the approach of summer come wild strawberries, plump peaches, cherries, figs and watermelons – all of which make you wonder why Venetian restaurant menus are so frequently uninspired.

Follow through into the Ruga degli Speziali, the street of the spice traders, where you may catch a whiff of fresh coffee beans and the few spices that are still sold from a couple of grocery stores. At the end of the street turn right for the **Pescheria**, or fish market (closed Sun

Above and Right: Campo di Rialto market stalls

and Mon), where gleaming sardines, sole and skate, sea bass and spider crabs, squid and live shrimps are all laid out in trays under the colonnades. Make for the far side of the market for good views of the Grand Canal and the *palazzi* on the far bank, including the Gothic gem of the Ca' d'Oro.

Walk alongside the fruit and vegetable market on your right, watch the produce being offloaded at the water's edge and carted off to stalls, shops and restaurants. High water permitting, wander along the quayside almost as far as the Rialto Bridge. Then rejoin the Ruga degli Orefici, passing the delightful **San Giacomo di Rialto**, the oldest church in Venice. Retrace your steps along to the Campo Beccarie and, if the mood takes you, stop for coffee at the rough and ready **Osteria da Pinto** where fishmongers may be having a morning tipple in the traditional *bacaro* (bar).

Follow the yellow signs for Piazzale Roma, which will take you over a bridge and into the Calle dei Botteri. Turn left here, ignore any yellow signs and follow the street until it narrows, at which point turn right into the little square marked Carampane. Pass under the *sottoportego*, then turn right into what is marked as the Rio Terà de la Carampane. The first bridge on your right is the **Ponte delle Tette** or Bridge of the Teats which, they say, is named after the prostitutes – of which there were over 11,000 in Venice in the 16th century – who used to frequent this quarter, stripping to the waist to lure their customers into the brothels.

Return to the street you came off and take the first right for the Campiello Albrizzi, a small square flanked on the far side by the well-preserved 18th-century Palazzo Albrizzi. Cross the square and turn left into what must be the narrowest alley in the city. Turn right under the colonnades and over the bridge into the Calle de la Furatola and you will soon reach the main Rialto/Piazzale Roma thoroughfare. Turn right into the Calle della Madon-

netta, cross the bridge and carry on until you come into the **Campo di San Polo**, the largest square in Venice after Piazza San Marco. It has none of the grandeur of San Marco but is nonetheless beautiful in its own busy way. Once the site of bullfights, tournaments, masked balls, fairs and festivals, it is now the scene of less exotic activities such as football and cycling.

Next to the church the Classical Palazzo Corner Mocenigo was for a while the residence of Frederick Rolfe (self-styled Baron Corvo), the notoriously eccentric English writer. It was here that he wrote *The Desire and Pursuit of the Whole*, ruthlessly lampooning English society in Venice. As a result his host threw him out, penniless, on to the streets. On the opposite side of the square is the Palazzo Soranzo with its sweeping pink Gothic façade. The most interesting feature of the church of **San Polo** is a chapel with Gian-domenico Tiepolo's paintings of the Stations of the Cross. Follow the sign for the *Crucis del Tiepolo*; if it is closed get the key from the sacristan.

Memorable Masks

Turn right out of the church, cross the bridge into the Calle dei Saoneri. If the **Trattoria Da Ignazio** (No 2749; closed Sat) appeals, book a table for lunch later on. The fish is excellent and there's a garden at the back. Small shops specialising in leather, lace, prints, masks and other Venetian crafts may tempt you along this and the next two streets. At the end of Calle dei Saoneri, turn left, past a print shop and then right into the Calle dei Nomboli. Half way along the stunning masks at **Tragicomica** invariably catch the attention of passers-by. Every one of them is handmade by craftsmen – hence the prices. Masks range from *Commedia dell'Arte* characters (Harlequin, Punch, etc) to allegorical masks of the creator's own invention. Almost opposite the shop is **Carlo Goldoni's house**, containing theatre memorabilia and relics of this great Venetian playwright.

Take the bridge at the end of the street and cross a small square to the Campo San Tomà. From here follow the signs for the Scuola Grande di San Rocco. This will bring you into the Campo dei Frari, dominated by the huge brick walls and soaring campanile of the **Frari church** (9am–6pm; closed Sun morning). Along with the church of Santi Giovanni e Paolo in Castello, this is the finest Gothic church in Venice. It was built in the 14th and 15th centuries by Franciscan friars whose first principle was poverty – hence the meagre decoration of the facade. You will need coins for the lighting and the recorded commentaries. Keep the ticket handy as it has on it a useful plan pinpointing the impressive art treasures contained in the church.

Once inside, the eye is inevitably drawn to Titian's gloriously rich *Assumption of the Virgin*, which crowns the main altar. On the entrance side of the church the same artist's *Madonna di Ca' Pesaro*, is another masterpiece of light, colour and harmony, and a very daring work in that it was one of the very earliest to depict the Madonna out of the centre of the composition. Members of the Pesaro family, who commissioned the work, can be seen in the lower half of the painting. Directly opposite is Titian's mausoleum, erected 300 years after his death. Other outstanding works of art are Giovanni Bellini's beautiful *Madonna and Child with Saints* in the

Above Left: San Giacomo di Rialto. **Left:** delivery boat on the Canal Grande
Right: festival mask

sacristy, of which Henry James said, 'Nothing in Venice is more perfect than this'; the finely carved 15th-century monks' choir; the wooden statue by Donatello of St John the Baptist on the altarpiece to the right of the main altar; and the sinister monument to Canova (to the left of the side door).

Works of Tintoretto

Turn right out of the church and follow the sign for the neighbouring **Scuola Grande di San Rocco** (open 9am–5.30pm). This fine Renaissance building contains an unrivalled collection of paintings by Tintoretto. He was one of several eminent contenders for the decoration of the Scuola, among them Veronese; but Tintoretto caught his competitors unaware by producing not merely a plan but a completed painting, already in place on the ceiling of the Conference Room. He worked on the Scuola on and off for 24 years.

On admission, collect a free plan of the paintings and a handy mirror for viewing the ceilings. As you go round note the artist's extraordinary ability to convey theatrical effect through contrasts of light and shade, bold foreshortening, visionary effects of colour and unusual viewpoints. In the lower hall the paintings illustrate scenes from the Life of the Virgin, while the upper hall has paintings over 4.8m (16ft) high depicting scenes from the Life of Christ and, on the ceiling, scenes from the Old Testament.

At the far end of the Sala dell'Albergo, scenes from the Passion culminate in *The Crucifixion* itself, fittingly the largest, most moving and dramatic painting of the collection. The *Glorification of St Roch* on the ceiling of the same room was the work which won Tintoretto the commission.

For lunch return to **Ignazio** *(see page 41)* or try **Da Fiore** north of the Campo San Polo *(see Eating Out, page 66)* in Calle del Scaleter 2202, an elegant little restaurant, off the beaten track and excellent for fish. If, after lunch, you feel like exploring the western part of the Dorsoduro return to the Campo San Rocco, take the Calle Fianco della Scuola beside the Scuola, then cross the bridge and walk to the end of the Calle della Scuola. Turn

Above: detail from Tintoretto's *The Last Supper*, Scuola Grande di San Rocco

left and immediately right into **Calle San Pantalon**, which brings you into the square of the same name. The church has a huge ceiling fresco by Fumiani. On the left-hand side of the square, close to the canal, spot the old slab which lists varieties of fish and the minimum sizes they had to reach before they were allowed to be sold. Cross the bridge over the Rio Foscari and walk to the **Campo di Santa Margherita**, a rectangular 'square' bustling with local life. **Causin** at the near end has particularly good ice creams.

The square tapers at the far end and brings you to the **church and Scuola of the Carmini** (Mon–Sat 9am–6pm, Sun 9am–4pm). The Scuola houses Tiepolo's sensational ceiling painting, *St Simon Stock Receiving the Scapular of the Carmelite Order from the Virgin*. The Carmelites were so pleased with it that they made Tiepolo an honorary member of the Scuola.

Coming back into the square keep to the right and follow the yellow signs for Accademia into the Rio Terrà Canal. Look out on the right for the mask shop **Mondonovo**. As you approach the canal of San Barnaba you will see, on the far side, one of the last floating vegetable markets. Cross the bridge into **Campo San Barnaba**, traditionally a quarter for the impoverished nobility. Look out for local craftsmen binding books and restoring antiques.

5. CIRCLING THE SERENISSIMA *(see map, p18–19)*

This circular tour around the periphery of Venice provides stunning views and will renew the spirits after an overdose of city sightseeing. In northern Venice visit the oldest ghetto in the world and the quarter of Madonna dell'Orto; complete the circle by returning via the Arsenale.

Catch a No 82 vaporetto from the San Zaccaria landing stage, east of Piazza San Marco and make sure it is going towards San Giorgio. Invest in a Day Pass for unlimited travel for 24 hours.

The boat veers out into the San Marco Canal towards the **island of San Giorgio Maggiore**. If you have not already seen the church and the views from its campanile, now is the time to do so. The boat will conveniently drop you right by the steps leading up to the church. The boat makes several stops on the **island of Giudecca**. This narrow, gently curving strip of land, made up of eight islands, serves as a suburb to Venice. Opinions differ as to the origins of the name, but it may stem from the word *giudicati* (meaning judged), dating from the days when troublesome aristocrats were banished here.

The island has a working fishing community, splendid views across to Venice and three churches of merit. The *vaporetto* stops at *Zitelle*, named after the nearby church of the same name, also

Right: the effect of San Giorgio Maggiore

designed by Palladio (now a conference centre). But the architect's most splendid church is the newly restored **Redentore** at the next stop. The great dome is one of the most conspicuous landmarks of Venice and the interior, strikingly stark and solemn, is a supreme example of Classical rationality. The church was built to commemorate the deliverance of Venice from the plague in 1576 which took 50,000 lives. Nearby is the pricey Harry's Dolci (*see Eating Out, page 66*).

Waterside wonders

After the Palanca stop, the boat crosses the Giudecca Canal to the **Zattere**. On a sunny day the quayside will lure you with its open-air cafés and views across to Giudecca. Stretch your legs along the quayside, see the Tiepolo ceiling in the **Gesuiti** church, then return to the landing stage to take waterbus No 52 towards the station (Ferrovia stop). At the western tip of Giudecca, before you leave the Giudecca Canal you can't fail to notice the massive neo-Gothic **Mulino Stucky**, formerly a flour mill, now being converted into a conference centre. The boat rounds the western end of Venice through docklands, then suddenly hits the Grand Canal. After the railway station you pass under the bridge of the Scalzi, then turn left up the Canale di Cannaregio, the main entrance into Venice before the advent of the Ponte della Libertà. Look left for **Palazzo Labia**, once home of the extraordinarily rich Labia family, now the headquarters of RAI, the broadcasting network.

Disembark at **Guglie**, the stop just after the stone and brick bridge. This is a lively area of Cannaregio with waterside stalls, small shops and trattorias. This northern arc of Venice, known as **Cannareggio**, is one of the most fascinating but least explored areas. The word *Cannareggio* comes from *canne*, meaning reeds and dates back to the days when all this territory was marshland. As you get off the boat turn left, go under the archway immediately on your right signposted Sinagoghe, which will take you past fascinating small workshops and bars to the **Ghetto Vecchio** and the **Campo della Scuola**. Continue over a bridge into the **Campo del Ghetto Nuovo**, which, despite its title, is in fact the world's oldest ghetto and the one that gave its name to Jewish communities around the world.

In the early 16th century Jews in Venice were confined to one of the islands of Cannaregio and the only answer to their cramped conditions was

to build upwards. Hence the 'skyscrapers' of Venice, tenement blocks of five or six storeys which used to be the highest blocks in Europe. The site was formerly an iron foundry where cannons were made and the word *ghetto* comes from *gettare* meaning to cast. The community remained on the site until 1797 when Napoleon had the gates torn down and from then on Jews could live wherever they liked in the city. Only a few Jewish families still live here.

The most striking feature of the large, rambling Campo del Ghetto Nuovo is the series of evocative bas-reliefs by Arbit Blatas, recording the Nazi holocaust. You will see them on the near side of the square, below symbolic strips of barbed wire. On the far side of the square you can visit the **Museo della Comunità Ebraica** (10am–5.30pm, closed Sat). Guided tours of the synagogues (English/Italian) leave at 30 minutes past the hour from 10.30am–3.30pm (or tel: 041-715359).

Take the northern exit from the square and cross the bridge into the Fondamenta degli Ormesini. Turn right along this bustling quayside, past small shops, bars and trattorias. Turn left down a narrow alley when you see the blue sign '*Ospedale*', cross the bridge and turn right along the pretty Fondamenta della Sensa. The cheap prices and picturesque canalside setting of the **Osteria alla Pergola** (tel: 041-720198) may tempt you to return here for lunch.

Follow the *fondamenta* as far as the **Campo dei Mori**. The statues here depict merchants of the Mastelli family who came to Venice from the Peloponnese in the 12th century. Following the waterside, past another turbaned merchant in a niche in the wall, to **Tintoretto's house** (Cannaregio No 3399), marked with a plaque and bas-relief of the artist, who lived here for many years. Return to the Campo dei Mori, cross the bridge on the far side and turn right for views of the relief of a one-legged man and a camel which has given this palace its popular name of the Palazzo del Cammello.

Retrace a few steps for the church of **Madonna dell'Orto** (Mon–Sat 10am–5pm, Sun 1–5pm), a masterpiece of Venetian Gothic, conspicuous for its oriental campanile, brick façade and carved portal. Inside it showcases Tintoretto paintings. It was the artist's parish church and he is buried in the first chapel on the right. Wander around this quiet neighbourhood where washing flaps in the breeze and cats doze in sunlit squares. *Orto* means kitchen garden and it is one of the few areas of Venice where gardens are a feature. Make for the Madonna dell'Orto landing stage on the northern embankment by taking the street west of the church.

Catch another No 52 *vaporetto* (clockwise direction) and change boats at the next stop, Fondamente Nuove. Here make sure you pick up Line 41/42 going in the direction

Left: the Redentore dome. **Above:** 'skyscrapers' in the Jewish ghetto. **Right:** the colossal lion guarding the Arsenale

of Tana/San Zaccaria. The boat speeds along the Fondamente Nuove, then swings sharp right, with a hoot, down into the **Arsenale** (where you can get off at the Tana stop to look around). This is the only way to see inside the walls of this once-splendid shipyard. Today it is hard to imagine the great galleys that were built here to protect Venice's maritime commerce.

Outside, the boat turns right and sweeps along the Riva degli Schiavoni, affording a splendid panorama of the classic perspectives of Venice, until it drops you at San Zaccaria.

6. THE ACCADEMIA GALLERY
– A FEAST OF VENETIAN ART *(see map, p20–1)*

'If only the Venetians learnt to draw at a young age…' remarked Michelangelo. They may not have been the greatest draughtsmen but Venetians knew how to paint. See for yourself in the Accademia gallery, the world's richest repository of Venetian art.

The paintings in the **Accademia** are dependent on natural light, so choose a bright morning and be at the gallery close to 9am (note the gallery closes at

2pm on Mon, 7pm on Sun and 7.30pm the rest of the week; currently it is open every day but it is best to check before you go). The later you leave it, the more crowded it will be, particularly in high season. The masterpieces, housed in the monastic complex of the Santa Maria della Carità, are too numerous to absorb in one visit and this itinerary concentrates on just some of the finest pictures. Before braving the queues, you might want to call in for a coffee and brioche at the **Belle Arti** café beside the gallery. Be prepared for whole rooms closed off for restoration. Look on the inside wall if you can't see the room number from the outside.

ROOM I shows the heavy influence of the Byzantine on the earliest Venetian painters. The principal exponent of the style in Venice was Paolo Veneziano. One of the most important of his works is the *Coronation of the Virgin* (freestanding, centre), a panel-painting (polyptych) with extravagant use of gold. Just before the steps up to Room II, look at the detailed rendering of figures in Michele Giambono's *Coronation of the Virgin* – a good example of the International Gothic style.

ROOM II contains one of the most important altarpieces of the early Venetian Renaissance: Giovanni Bellini's *Madonna Enthroned with Saints* (right wall). Renaissance painting came late to Venice, brought largely through the great genius Mantegna. Giovanni Bellini was his brother-in-law and he, in turn, influenced all the Venetian painters of his own and the following generation. Bellini broke away from the traditional polyptych and brought

Above: *Madonna of the Little Trees* by Giovanni Bellini. **Above Right:** *St John the Baptist* by Titian. **Right:** *Corpus Domini Procession* in the Accademia by Gentile Bellini

the Virgin and saints together in a single natural composition. This painting had an important influence on Vittore Carpaccio's *Presentation of Jesus in the Temple* and Marco Basaiti's *Christ Praying in the Garden*, both hanging in the same room. All three were painted for the church of San Giobbe.

Skip Room III and concentrate on the gems in **ROOM IV** and **ROOM V**. Giovanni Bellini was the greatest of the Venetian Madonna painters. His *Madonna and Child with St Catherine and St Mary Magdalene* (on the right as you go in) demonstrates his masterly balance of naturalness, reality and beauty. In the same room (left wall as you go in) Mantegna's *St George* typifies the dry rationality of the artist's *quattrocento* style. Follow through into **ROOM V** for further masterpieces by Giovanni Bellini, including the lovely *Madonna of the Little Trees* and *Madonna and Child with John the Baptist and a Saint*. In his evocative *Pietà*, Bellini makes striking use of landscape.

In the same room is one of the very great works of the Venetian Renaissance: *The Tempest* by Giorgione. Little is known about the artist, who died of the plague when very young, but he is ranked as one of the founders of modern painting. Giorgione was an innovator in that he achieved his effect through the use of colour and light as opposed to line and drawing. *The Tempest* is one of the artist's few certain attributions, but the subject still remains a mystery. Beside it, *The Old Woman* by the same artist is a striking piece of early realism.

Turn left for **ROOM VI.** This and the adjoining **ROOMS VII** and **VIII** concentrate on the early 16th century when the Venetian Renaissance was into its stride. In **ROOM VI**, Titian boldly presents *St John the Baptist* as a muscular athlete in a theatrical pose. After the death of Giorgione (1510), Titian (*circa* 1487–1576) went on to dominate Venetian painting throughout his long life. Brilliant use of colour and lyrical composition are the ingredients of his genius. Typical of the first half of the 16th century are the richly coloured, exuberant paintings such as *The Presentation of the Ring* by Paris Bordone (**ROOM VI**) and the *Sacra Conversazione* by **Palma Il Vecchio** in (**ROOM VIII**). On an entirely different note is the melancholy and penetrating *Portrait of a Young Man* by **Lorenzo Lotto** in **ROOM VII**, left wall. Acute observation of personality is a feature of Venetian Renaissance portraiture.

Three Great Masters

Take the steps up to **ROOM X** where three of the greatest Venetian masters are represented. To your right and covering the entire wall is Veronese's grandiose *Feast in the House of Levi*. It was painted as *The Last Supper* but its hedonistic content (dogs, drunkards, dwarfs, etc) brought Veronese before the Inquisition. Rather than eliminate the offending details, however, the painter merely changed the title.

Tintoretto (1518–94) was born in Venice and, unlike Titian, never moved from her shores. A man of fanatical religious conviction, he brought a kind of frenetic Mannerism to the Renaissance. His reputation was made with the striking *St Mark Rescuing the Slave* which you see on the opposite wall as you go in. Inspired use of shadow, foreshortening, depth and movement are typified in the dramatic *Stealing of the Body of St Mark* and *St Mark saving a Saracen from Shipwreck*. In the same room, Titian's dark sober *Pietà*, bathed in mystic light, was the artist's last work.

ROOM XI displays some sumptuous works by Veronese. The *Marriage of St Catherine* and *Madonna Enthroned with Saints* are radiant, richly coloured works demonstrating his use of dazzling hues. At the end of the room you can't miss Tiepolo's grandiose *tondo*, *Discovery of the True Cross*, showing his mastery of illusionistic perspective.

ROOM XII is a gallery of light-hearted, lyrical, almost sugary landscape paintings. During the 18th century the key note in art was to delight and please the senses. Good examples are the graceful, airy *Rape of Europa* and *Apollo and Marsia* by **Tiepolo** (**ROOM XVI**). As a young man Tiepolo was influenced by **Piazzetta**, whose dashing use of *chiaroscuro* in free-handling style is seen in his masterpiece, *The Soothsayer* (**ROOM XVIA**).

Topographical painting, as illustrated in **ROOM XVII**, was a fashion of the

Above: *The Tempest* by Giorgione
Right: Ca' d'Oro, the sumptuous Palace of Gold

time. Antonio Canal, better known as Canaletto, transformed the fashion into an industry. *Perspective* is a good example of his precisely drawn scenes. For an intimate insight into Venetian daily life in the 18th century take a look at Pietro Longhi's witty genre paintings towards the end of the room.

Now you go back in time. Three left turns should bring you to **ROOM XX** containing eight large canvases by five 'ceremonial artists' of the late 15th/early 16th century, commissioned by the *Scuole Grande di San Giovanni Evangelista*. The scenes, depicting stories of *The True Cross,* are full of historical detail, documenting Venetian life in the 15th century. Worth singling out are the *Corpus Domini Procession* by Gentile Bellini showing Piazza San Marco at the end of the 15th century and the *The Curing of a Man possessed by Demons* by Carpaccio, showing the old wooden Rialto bridge which collapsed in 1444. Go back through ROOM XIX and turn left, past the book shop for the last room, **ROOM XXIV**. On the right the great tryptych of Antonio Vivarini and Giovanni d'Alemagna demonstrates a combination of the International Gothic and the emerging Renaissance styles. Facing you Titian's *The Presentation of the Virgin*, still occupying its original position on the entrance wall of the gallery, makes a fitting finale to your visit.

7. PALACES ON THE GRAND CANAL *(see map, p20–1)*

Have you ever wondered what it was like to live on the Grand Canal? This morning's tour of three *palazzi* converted to museums will give you some idea. Ensure you have a boat ticket.

Your morning starts at the **Ca' d'Oro** (8.15am–2pm daily), the most magnificent Gothic palace in Venice. From San Marco it is the first stop on a No. 1 *vaporetto* after the Rialto. The lace-like façade with its ogee windows, carved capitals, crowning pinnacles and bas-reliefs was once covered in gold leaf – hence the name, House of Gold. From the landing stage take the narrow *calle* and you will see the entrance to the gallery on the left. Pause in the picturesque main courtyard with the open stairway and Bartolomeo Bon's beautifully carved red Verona marble well-head. Of the Re-

naissance masterpieces on the first floor of the gallery, Franchetti's most prized piece was Mantegna's *St Sebastian*. Also worth singling out is Tullio Lombardo's delightful marble double portrait. At the far end the *portego* provides fine views of the Grand Canal. Move on in time to the second floor where you can see fresco fragments by Giorgione and Titian – moved from the Fondaco dei Tedeschi for preservation.

The next palazzo, the **Ca' Rezzonico**, takes you into the 18th century. Though entire ceilings and many of the furnishings have been taken from other palaces it looks very authentic and gives an idea of what life was like in those hedonistic days. Six stops on the *vaporetto* (direction San Marco) will bring you to the Ca' Rezzonico landing stage. Just before the stop you can't miss the vast façade of the palace, with its columns, arcades, balconies and

abundance of sculptural detail. To get there from the landing stage, take the Calle del Traghetto to the Campo Santa Barnaba. Stop for coffee in the square, watch the local life and morning shoppers scurrying to the floating vegetable market. Afterwards, cross the bridge nearest the church and turn right for the *palazzo*, marked *Museo del Settecento Veneziano* (Museum of 18th-Century Venice).

Palatial Splendour

The palace was designed in 1667 by the only great Venetian baroque architect, Baldassare Longhena, and later bought by the fabulously rich Rezzonico family. At one time it was owned by Robert Browning's reprobate son, Pen, and his wealthy American heiress wife – and it was while Robert Browning was staying here with them that he died of bronchitis. The interior of the palace is suitably grandiose. A formidable stone stairway leads up to the splendid ballroom with massive gilt chandeliers and frescoed ceilings. Beyond are a series of stately rooms embellished by frescoed ceilings, ostentatious vase stands and lacquered furniture. From the balcony at the end there are fine views of the Grand Canal.

The second floor is a picture gallery of 18th-century Venetian paintings. Don't miss the scenes by Longhi and the paintings of carnival and clowns by Domenico Tiepolo. If the palace is closed for restoration, consider visiting the Accademia, further down the Grand Canal – *see page 46.*)

If there is time and energy for another *palazzo*, opt for something entirely different: the eccentric **Palazzo Venier dei Leoni** (10am–6pm, Sat until 10pm, closed Tues) containing the Guggenheim Collection. It is not far by foot from the Ca' Rezzonico; alternatively go one stop on the *vaporetto*, turn left when disembarking at *Accademia* and follow the signs. With its unfinished neoclassical façade (it is known as the Palazzo Nonfinito) the structure could not look less like a Venetian *palazzo*. Peggy Guggenheim, the eccentric American art lover, bought the palace in 1949 and lived here until she died in 1979. Her collection is all 20th century, with the emphasis

Above: statue in the courtyard of Ca' Rezzonico

city itineraries

on Surrealism. The majority of the works came directly from the artists, whom she befriended, patronised, entertained or – in the case of Max Ernst – married. She is buried here behind the *palazzo* with her dogs.

Whether or not you visit the Guggenheim, the Dorsoduro is a good area to stay for lunch – either a snack on the Zattere or a meal at one of two restaurants between the Guggenheim and the Accademia: **Agli Alboretti** or **Ai Cugnai** *(see Eating Out, page 67).*

8. TORCELLO – RELIC OF FORMER GLORY *(see map, p52)*

Leave the splendour of La Serenissima for a tiny island on the lagoon. Lunch at a famous 'locanda' or rustic trattoria, then visit the surviving sights of this once flourishing island (ferry No 12).

You can either take the No 12 ferry from Fondamente Nuove or take the far slower No 14 all the way from San Zaccaria, stopping en route at the Lido, Punta Sabbioni, Treporti and Burano. Avoid Sunday in summer if at all possible.

It is hard to believe that the flat little island of Torcello, whose inhabitants number around 70, was once the centre of a thriving civilisation. In its heyday the Torcello's population was around 20,000, but as Venice rose to power, decline and decay set in. Trade dwindled, the waters silted up and spread. Today, the cathedral, church and a couple of *palazzi* are the sole evidence of former splendour. It is a lonely, nostalgic and – if you are in the mood – romantic island.

From afar you can spot the campanile of the cathedral rising above the flat marshland. From the landing stage follow the island's only 'road'

Above: time out for a daydream
Right: open-air lace stall

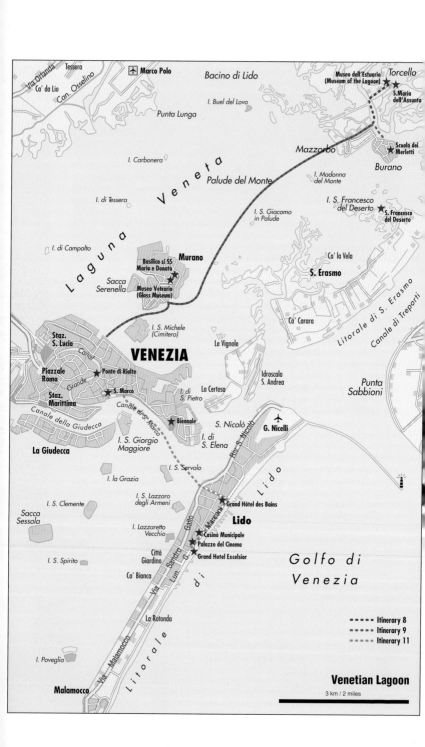

Marco Polo

Bacino di Lido

Tessera

Via Orlanda

Ca' da Lio

Con. Osselino

Punta Lunga

I. Buel del Lovo

Museo dell'Estuario
(Museum of the Lagoon)

Torcello

S.Maria
dell'Assunta

I. Carbonera

Mazzorbo

Scuola dei
Merletti

Burano

L a g u n a   V e n e t a

Palude del Monte

I. Madonna
del Monte

I. di Tessera

I. S. Giacomo
in Palude

I. S. Francesco
del Deserto

S. Francesco
del Deserto

I. di Campalto

Basilica si SS
Maria e Donato

Murano

Ca' la Vela

S. Erasmo

Sacca
Serenella

Museo Vetrario
(Glass Museum)

Ca' Carara

Litorale di S. Erasmo

Canale di Treporti

Staz.
S. Lucia

Canal

I. S. Michele
(Cimitero)

Le Vignole

Piazzale
Roma

Grande

Ponte di Rialto

VENEZIA

La Certosa

Idroscalo
S. Andrea

Punta
Sabbioni

Staz.
Marittima

Canale di S. Marco

S. Marco

I. di
S. Pietro

Canale della Giudecca

Biennale

S. Nicolò

G. Nicelli

La Giudecca

I. S. Giorgio
Maggiore

I. di
S. Elena

Riv. S. Nicolò

I. la Grazia

I. S. Servolo

L i d o

Sacca
Sessola

I. S. Clemente

I. S. Lazzaro
degli Armeni

Grand Hôtel des Bains

Marconi

Lido

I. Lazzaretto
Vecchio

Casinò Municipale
Palazzo del Cinema

Grand Hotel Excelsior

G o l f o   d i

Città
Giardino

Sandara

Lung. G.

Via

Ca' Bianca

V e n e z i a

I. S. Spirito

La Rotonda

Via   Malamocco

L i t o r a l e   d i

I. Poveglia

Malamocco

- - - - - Itinerary 8
- - - - - Itinerary 9
- - - - - Itinerary 11

Venetian Lagoon

3 km / 2 miles

city itineraries

– a rustic path beside a narrow canal. It all seems extraordinarily quiet and rural in comparison to the city.

In the Footsteps of the Famous

If you lunch at the **Locanda Cipriani** *(see Eating Out, page 66)* you will be following in the footsteps of Hemingway (who once spent a winter here shooting duck in the lagoon and completing his book *Across the River and into the Trees*), Queen Elizabeth II, Sir Winston Churchill, Charlie Chaplin and Sophia Loren. The Locanda, which has just five bedrooms, is run by the Cipriani family of Harry's Bar fame. Like its parent establishment it prides itself on its wonderful home-made pastas, *carpaccio* (thin slices of raw fillet of beef) and its *dolci*. Prices are on the high side but the place itself is unpretentious and quiet; on a warm day you can sit on the terrace overlooking gardens, church and cathedral. A less pricey alternative is the pleasantly rural **Al Ponte del Diavolo** (on the left before you get to the centre; see *Eating Out, page 68*).

After lunch, you might want to browse through the open-air stalls selling lace and linen, run by little old ladies, then start your sightseeing where the settlement began in the **Cathedral of Santa Maria Assunta** (10am–5.30pm daily). This was started as early as AD 639 but was rebuilt between the 9th and 11th centuries. Note the foundations of the original baptistry on your left as you enter and the massive stone slabs acting as shutters on the south side of the cathedral, dating from the 11th century.

The interior – simple, spacious, light and dignified – is impressive and its lovely mosaics are among the oldest and finest in Italy.

Above and Right: interior and exterior details of the Cathedral of Santa Maria Assunta

Most striking of all is *The Virgin and Child*, set against a glowing gold background in the dome of the central apse.

Covering the western wall is *The Last Judgement*, a massive mosaic full of narrative. From this end admire the church in its entirety: the slender marble columns, the wooden tie-beams, and the roodscreen carved with peacocks, lions and flowers, surmounted by a frieze of 15th-century paintings.

The church of **Santa Fosca**, adjoining the cathedral via a pretty portico, was built in the 11th century to enshrine the body of Santa Fosca, the Christian martyr. Close to the church, the primitive stone chair, known as *Attila's Seat*, was once said to have been used by the king of the Huns. A more likely theory is that it was used by the island tribunes. According to local folklore if you sit on the chair you will be married within the year.

On the opposite side of the piazza, the *Palazzo dell'Archivio and Palazzo del Consiglio* have been restored to house the **Museo dell'Estuario** (Museum of the Lagoon); (closed Mon) containing archaeological finds from the the earliest days of Torcello's history. The ferries back to Venice leave fairly regularly. Since the boats go back via Burano, you may like to spend an hour or so there before the return trip to Venice *(see below)*.

9. A BOAT TO BURANO *(see map, p52)*

Burano is the most colourful of the islands in the lagoon. The waterways are bordered by brightly coloured houses, streets are lined with stalls selling lace and linen and the fishing and boatbuilding communities are very much in evidence. Spend the afternoon here, relaxing perhaps after a morning's serious sightseeing in Venice – or combine it with a trip to Torcello and/or Murano (ferry No 12 or 14).

Ferry No 12 for Burano leaves from the Fondamente Nuove every hour and takes 40–50 minutes, or you can catch the slower No 14 all the way from San Zaccaria. Avoid summer weekends when the boats are packed to capacity.

If you choose to go to the island in time for lunch, there are plenty of very pleasant open-air *trattorias* specialising in fish. Ferries for Burano depart from the landing stage by the bridge near the Gesuiti church. Arrive in good

time to get a seat on the upper deck. Sit on the right-hand side for the best views of the islands of the lagoon.

The first you pass is the cemetery island of **San Michele** where several illustrious former visitors to Venice are buried. The boat will stop at **Murano**, centre of the Venetian glass-making industry since the end of the 13th century. Spot the *fornaci* (furnaces) as you go by. From here the ferry will head out into the lagoon for the more remote islands, passing through a channel delineated by piles where seagulls perch. On your right for most of the journey you can see the marshy islets and main island of **Sant'Erasmo**, where fruit and vegetables are grown for Venetian consumption. To the left, in the distance, planes will be taking off and landing at Marco Polo airport. The ferry swings left around the deserted island of San Giacomo in Palude, one of many islands abandoned in the 1960s. To the right, in the distance a dark cluster of cypresses marks the romantic island of San Francesco del Deserto.

Island Approach

As you get closer to Burano you will see its leaning campanile. The ferry soon enters the canal of **Mazzorbo**, the little island linked to Burano by a footbridge. Once a flourishing centre of the lagoon, Mazzorbo is now a backwater of orchards, gardens and one enticing trattoria. The only surviving church on the island is the Romanesque/Gothic Santa Caterina. Burano

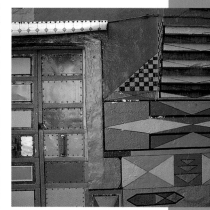

strikes you as lively and colourful after a trip through the desolate lagoon. About 5,000 people live here, many of them fishermen or glass workers who commute to the factories of Murano. Take away the canals and it looks and feels something like a Greek island.

From the landing stage, follow the general flow past souvenir stalls and painted houses where you may see ladies busily embroidering at the front doors. Explore the island at leisure – it is small enough to do so. If you are planning to eat, do so in the Via Baldassare Galuppi, the main street of the island, named after the composer who was born here. The restaurant with the best reputation (and hence the highest prices) is an ex-haunt of artists, the **Trattoria da Romano** (closed Tues; tel: 041-730030) on the left at No 221. Stick to fish – either as *antipasto*, in soup or freshly grilled – and you are unlikely to be disappointed.

To view the most colourful *cortile* (courtyard) on the island, take the tiny alley opposite the Galuppi restaurant in the same street. Casa Bepi at No 339 has a multicoloured geometrical façade which truly dazzles the eye. The ubiquitous **lace and linen** stalls and shops all vie for attention. There are some reasonable purchases to be had among the tablecloths, napkins and blouses, but don't be fooled into thinking it is all handmade on Burano. Virtually all is factory-made in Asia and the prices on the island are the same as those in Venice itself. In the 16th century, Venetian, and particularly Burano, lace

Left: a typical scene on Burano, the most colourful of the lagoon's islands
Right: the brightly painted facade of Casa Bepi

varini – named after the 15th-century family of painters who lived on Murano. From the bridge you can see the **Palazzo da Mula** (on the far bank to your right), one of Murano's few surviving grand mansions. At the far side of the bridge, and left along the Rio dei Vetrai stands the church of **San Pietro Martire**, which contains altarpieces by Giovanni Bellini.

Further along, the Fondamenta is more or less given over to glass factories, glass shops and glass showrooms. Many pieces in the shops are from the Far East and it is difficult to tell what is made in Murano and what is not. On the other side of the canal visit the **Museum of 20th-Century Murano Glass** to see some stylish contemporary pieces *(see Shopping/glassware, page 63)*. And if you haven't seen a glass-blowing display, stop at one of the workshops. With incredible skill the craftsman blows the heated glass paste into the desired form, then with a spatula and pair of pincers, twists, turns, pinches and flattens it into a perfect shape. The landing stage for boats back to Venice lies at the end of the Rio dei Vetrai. Boats going to Torcello *(see Itinerary 8, page 51)* stop at the Faro landing stage east of the *rio*.

11. BEACH BREAK AT THE LIDO *(see map, p52)*

Leave the sights of the city, catch a '*vaporetto*' to Venice's main bathing resort and cool off in the waters of the Adriatic. Avoid summer Sundays when all Venetians go.

Unless you are affluent enough to go by gondola or motor launch, take a No 1, 52, 82, 6 or 14 boat from the Riva degli Schiavoni (1, 42, 52, 62 and 82 also go from the Piazzale Roma), No 6 being direct. Public boats link the Lido to the city, leaving about every four minutes. If you want to try your luck at the summer casino, which opens at 3pm; take your passport for ID and line your pockets with lire.

The 11km (7 mile) strip of land protecting the Venetian lagoon from the Adriatic Sea was Italy's first *lido*. In the 19th century romantics came es-

cape the city, to walk or ride along the sands and swim. By the turn of the 20th century it was one of the most fashionable resorts of Europe and the name was subsequently applied to dozens of bathing resorts throughout the world. The Lido may have lost some of its cachet since the days of Visconti's film *Death in Venice*, but the beach still provides an essential cooling-off experience on a scorching hot day. If you are with children, a trip here will be top priority. The ferry ride across the lagoon, which only takes 12 or 20 minutes (depending on which boat you take) is fun in itself.

You arrive on the Lido at the Piazzale Santa Maria Elisabetta. From here take the Gran Viale Santa Maria Elisabetta, the main road leading to the beaches and tourist office. Cars, buses and taxis come as something of a shock if you have already acclimatised yourself to the traffic-free streets of Venice.

Follow the street to the far end where you can look over the beach from the Piazzale Bucintoro. Turn right for the **Lungomare G Marconi**, the boulevard boasting the best hotels and beaches. The only public beaches are the strips either end, which, being free, are inevitably the least desirable.

You can treat yourself to a beach hut with comfortable sunbeds provided by hotels which have concessions on the beach, but these do not come cheap. You cannot do much better than the beach opposite the Grand Hôtel des Bains, where the sand is manicured daily *(see below)*. Otherwise keep to the sand nearest to the water's edge, where no one can turf you off. Dubious Italian surveys have found the waters at the Lido to be among the cleanest along the Adriatic coast. Judge for yourself.

Littoral landmarks

The **Hôtel des Bains** is the Lido's most famous landmark, immortalised by Thomas Mann and Luchino Visconti (*Death in Venice* was filmed here). Further along, the **Palazzo del Casinò** and **Palazzo del Cinema**, where the International Film Festival is held each summer, are typical of the Fascist architecture of the 1930s. Another landmark, the **Excelsior Hotel** is an exuberant piece of late 19th/early 20th century, neo-Byzantine architecture *(also see Accommodation, page 87)*.

The Lido is Venice's main centre for sport. Ask at the Excelsior Hotel about tickets for non-residents at the Lido Venice Club, which offers a wide range of sporting possibilities, including watersports, riding, tennis and golf. If you would rather take to the skies, the *Aeroclub di Venezia* at San Nicolò airport, offers hour-long flights over Venice. Time your return trip as the sun is setting. The approach to San Marco via San Giorgio Maggiore is an experience you are unlikely to forget.

Right and Above: time to relax on the sands of the Lido

down into the Ruga degli Orefici, street of the goldsmiths, where jewellers have hung out for centuries. Best buys in the Rialto area are silk ties, soft leather wallets, lambs wool and angora sweaters.

Turn left into the Ruga Vecchia San Giovanni, and follow the main flow going in the Piazzale Roma direction. Catch wafts of homemade bread as you pass food shops and *trattorias*. Carry on past a variety of shops into the busy Campo San Aponal. Cross the square, following the signs for the Piazzale Roma, into a tiny alley where a shop on the right sells miniature silver gondolas, tortoises and frogs.

Carry on to the lovely Campo di San Polo where children will be out playing. Follow the signs for the Piazzale Roma, go straight on into Calle Saoneri, with some fascinating specialist shops. At **Amadi Bruni**, No 2747, you may see a craftsman making tiny glass mice or spiders.

Turning left at the end you will pass a shop with a large choice of prints of Venice. In the Calle dei Nomboli which follows, the exotic carnival and theatre masks at **Tragicomica** (daily 10am–1pm, 3–7pm) are sure to catch your eye.

Just before you come into the Campo San Tomà, follow the yellow sign for the *traghetto*. If you haven't been on a gondola now is the time to do so. These ferry services cross the canal at half a dozen points. Step on board, pay the small fee and trust the gondolier to weave his way deftly through the traffic along the Grand Canal. Once off the boat take the narrow street ahead, then walk to the end of the Piscina San Samuele. Take a left turn into Calle degli Botteghe which will bring you face to face with the church of Santo Stefano. Turn right into the square and take the narrow street marked to San Marco.

On your way back to Piazza San Marco you will be passing some of the smartest shops in the city. In the Calle del Spezier by Ponte San Maurizio, you may well be delayed by the **Pasticceria Marchini** which has an irresistible selection of cakes, pastries and multicoloured chocolate. In Campo Maurizio two shops sell exotic fabrics, some with Fortuny designs.

In Campiello della Feltrina, **Legatoria Piazzesi** (tel: 041-5221202) has a wonderful selection of hand-printed paper, with distinctive marble designs. You can see the antique woodblocks which are still used to make them by the traditional *carta varese* method. There is plenty of scope for gifts here: decorative boxes, frames, albums, sketch books and card games.

Among the big names in fashion are Armani, Valentino, Laura Biagiotti and Missoni, all with eye-catching windows. The **Calle Larga XXII Marzo** and the streets between here and Piazza San Marco are the smartest shopping addresses in town. Try **Osvaldo Böhm** in the Salizzada San Moisè for prints, etchings and watercolours of Venice, or **Fantoni**, in Salizzada San Luca, for art books.

In Calle Vallaresso on the right before you get to Piazza San Marco, **Camiceria San Marco** will make you made-to-measure shirts, dresses and pyjamas within 24 hours. Slightly more off-beat and fun is the street called **Frezzeria** running north of the Salizzada San Moisè.

A fitting end to the day is **Piazza San Marco** whose arcades shelter luxury jewellers, hand-embroidered linen and lace and costly pieces of glass.

After exploring the San Marco and Mercerie shopping area, you may find yourself in the mood for hunting down specific gifts or *objets d'art*.

Although bargains rarely exist in Venice, the more fortunate will come away with

Left: marbled paper

exquisite fabrics, designer clothes, shoes that fit like a glove, and unique, hand-crafted items. Few visitors leave without a requisite supply of at least one Venetian craft, whether carnival masks or hand-blown Murano glassware, a distinctly gaudy but popular buy.

Fabrics

The luxurious fabrics made by the Spanish-born Mario Fortuny have outlasted lesser fads. In his Giudecca factory a century ago, he produced jewel-coloured velvets and bold silks inspired by original Renaissance costumes.

The Venetian factory still produces fabrics created according to Fortuny designs, and these are only on sale here. Equally fine are the reels of velvets, damasks and brocades created by the family firm of Bevilacqua, who work on the same 18th-century wooden looms they used when the firm first started.

Antichita V Trois, Campo San Maurizio (tel: 041-5222905) has the sole right to sell Fortuny fabrics.

Gaggio, Campo Santo Stefano, San Marco 3451 (open until 7.30pm, closed Sunday; tel: 041-5228574). The company is widely renowned for printing Art Deco designs on silk and velvet fabrics. (San Samuele *vaporetto* stop).

Luigi Bevilacqua, Campiello della Comare, Santa Croce 1320 (open 9am–6pm, closed Sunday; tel: 041-5242302/721566)

is the other place for hand-crafted fabrics (San Toma *vaporetto* stop).

Masks

It is particularly good fun to visit the mask workshops in the run up to carnival, when masks are being ordered and tried on. These colourful carnival masks can adorn a wall as well as a face.

The following are two authentic yet lively places that specialise in both theatrical and carnival masks.

Ca' del Sol, Fondamenta Osmarin, off Campo San Zaccaria (tel: 041-5285549).

Laboratorio Artigiano Maschere, Barberie delle Tole, Castello 6657 (closed Sunday).

Glassware

The great names of Venetian glassware tend to have an outlet in central Venice, although their factories and main showrooms are always on the island of Murano.

Barovier & Toso, Fondamenta Vetrai 28, Murano (tel: 041-739049) is a long-established firm with an international reputation for artistry. Visitors can also view their glass museum (open weekdays only), set on the top floor of the 16th-century palace that doubles as their showrooms and headquarters.

Venini, Piazzetta Leoncini 314, off Piazza San Marco, is one of the most reputable firms, and even produces witty glass versions of traditional masks.

If you wish to watch the whole process of glass-making, then visit the Murano factory

Above: Venetian carnival mask

and showrooms (Venini, Fondamenta Vetrai 50, Murano; tel: 041-739955).

Shoes & Leatherware

Shoes, bags and belts are produced not far from Venice, on the Brenta Riviera, which is home to the most important leather factories in northern Italy. Although not cheap, shoes and bags generally represent good quality buys, and usually come in stylish, classic designs rather than following the latest designer fashions.

Most such shops tend to be in the San Marco, Mercerie and Rialto areas. As far as leatherware and clothes are concerned, the most exclusive shopping area is Via XXII Marzo and the streets around Piazza San Marco. In theory, prices tend to be lower towards the Rialto Bridge, but much depends on the individual shop.

Calzaturificio Magli, Calle Larga XXII Marzo, San Marco 2288 (tel: 041-5208280)
Mariani Italo, Calle Teatro Goldini, San Marco 4775 (tel: 041-5235580)
Rossetti, Campo San Salvador, San Marco 4800 (tel: 041-5230571).

Off the Beaten Track

Shopping in the city of Venice does not have to involve only the elegant Piazza San Marco, Salizzada San Moisè and Calle Larga XXII Marzo, or the strange little corners of the Mercerie. It is rewarding to leave the main streets and just wander about. The curious will come across small galleries, old bookshops and perhaps even some precious prints.

EATING OUT

Despite their past trade in exotic spices and foods, Venetians never seem to have really excelled gastronomically. The mainstay of their diet has nearly always been fish fresh from the lagoon and rice from the Po valley. Venetian specialities are limited and hardly adventurous. Those you find most frequently are *risi e bisi* (rice and peas cooked with onion, ham and herbs in a chicken stock), *pasta e fagioli* (pasta and bean soup) and *fegato alla veneziana* (thinly sliced calves' liver with sauté onions and slabs of grilled *polenta*). The mediocrity of much Venetian cuisine, coupled with high costs, often leads to disappointment when it comes to dining out.

There are, of course, exceptions and sufficient of them to keep the brief visitor satisfied. The restaurants in the itineraries have been handpicked for excellence of quality and (by Venetian standards) value. Listed overleaf are several more, starting with the well-known gastronomic venues where you pay an arm and a leg for the very best, to off-the-beaten-track cheap family-run trattorias and cafés. The simple rule to avoid the highest prices – whether it's a cup of coffee or a five-course blow-out – is to steer clear of San Marco. To avoid all the hidden extras such as cover charge (L4,000–10,000) and service (10–15 percent) opt for the set menus. These start at around L35,000 for a three-course inclusive meal. The cheapest eating tends to be in the north of the city, in

restaurants

and around Cannareggio or the San Giacomo dall'Orio area in Santa Croce. Often an *antipasto* followed by a pasta or rice dish (eg *prosciutto* and melon, followed by fish *risotto*) is more enjoyable and works out cheaper than a main meat or fish course.

Fish features on virtually every menu; if you are lucky it will be that morning's catch. Most of the fish, either displayed outside restaurants or at the Rialto fish market, is caught a long way from the lagoon and prices are far from reasonable. A seafood antipasto (*antipasto di mare*) could put you back L25,000 lire and a plate of grilled mixed fish (*grigliata mista di pesce*) L25,000–40,000. Among the fish and seafood you are likely to come across are sole, sea bass, turbot, mullet, San Pietro (a tasty white fish), crayfish, crab, cuttle fish and squid.

Also worth trying are *granseoli*, sea spiders from Yugoslavia, served cold with lemon and olive oil; or *moleche*, small crabs caught as they are changing their shells, fried with oil, garlic and herbs. You can eat the shell and pincers too.

Pasta comes in all sizes and colours. Try the local speciality, *bigoli* – black strands of spaghetti made with wholewheat flour, served perhaps with an anchovy or tuna sauce. Practically any pasta served with seafood is a safe bet. Look out for pastas *alla vongole* (with clams), *ai frutti di mare* (with shell fish) or *alla marinara* (with mixed seafood). The favourite dessert is *tiramisù* (literally 'pick-me-up') – a creamy, alcoholic coffee and chocolate gâteau.

Wine

The house wine, *vino della casa*, is usually perfectly drinkable, and often very pleasant. It is likely to be a dry white Tocai or a dry Cabernet or Merlot (reds), all from the Friuli region to the north of Venice. In the cheaper establishments wine will be served in litre or half-litre carafes or jugs. You are also bound to come across the familiar names from the Veneto – Valpolicella, Bardolino and Soave.

As a refreshing aperitif there is little to beat a glass of Prosecco or Cartizzi, good quality sparkling white wines from the Veneto. Many Venetians also drink them with their meals.

Expensive Restaurants
Over L150,000

For setting, there is little to beat the top-floor restaurant of the Danieli Hotel and the terrace of the Gritti Palace, with wonderful views over the Grand Canal *(see Hotels, page 82–3)*. At all the restaurants listed here it is wise to make reservations in advance.

Ae Poste Vecie
Pescheria (Fish Market)
San Polo 1608
Tel: 041-721822
San Silvestro vaporetto stop.
Open for lunch and dinner; last orders at 9 or 9.30pm. Closed Tuesday.
By the fish market close to the Rialto Bridge, this is a well-established seafood restaurant, in a 16th-century palace. The chef prides himself on recreating dishes eaten during the glory days of the Serene Republic, including seafood *risotto*, seafood grills, and *baccala mantecato* (cod paste on toast).

Al Covo
Campiello della Pescheria
Riva degli Schiavoni
Castello 3968
Tel: 041-5223812
Arsenale or San Zaccaria vaporetto stops.
Open for lunch and dinner, except on Wednesday and Thursday.
Ideal for a sophisticated, candlelit dinner. Offers a subtle selection of seafood dishes. The desserts are also renowned.

Al Graspo De Ua
Calle dei Bombaseri
Campo San Bartolomeo
Tel: 041-5200150
Rialto vaporetto stop.
Open for lunch and dinner until 11pm, except on Monday.
Set beside the Rialto bridge, this renowned restaurant is equally good at fish and meat dishes. Friendly staff.

Antico Martini
Campo San Fantin
San Marco 1983
Tel: 041-5224121
Santa Maria del Etiglio vaporetto stop.
Closed Tuesday and lunchtime Wednesday.

Save this recommendation for an extra spe-
cial occasion. The cuisine (international and
classic Italian) rates among the finest in
Venice. A charming setting and an elegant
clientele, despite the sluggish rebuilding of
the nearby Fenice opera house.

Da Fiore
Calle del Scaleter
San Polo 2202a
Tel: 041-721308
San Silvestro vaporetto stop.
Closed Sunday and Monday.
Inconspicuous, elegant and excellent for fish.
Dull décor but a cosy bar. Above average
service. Popular with Americans.

Da Franz
Fondamenta San Giuseppe
Castello 754
Tel: 041-5220861
Closed Tuesday and January.
Off the beaten track, close to the public gar-
dens, Da Franz is an excellent choice for
seafood. Lots of locals. Serves variations
on Venetian classics; summer terrace over-
looks the canal.

Do Leoni
Londra Palace
Riva degli Schiavoni
Castello 4171
Tel: 041-5200533
Set by the San Zaccaria ferry stop.
This authentic restaurant offers Venetian del-
icacies in an elegant ambience overlooking
the island of San Giorgio. It is popular with
the Venetians themselves, proof that the food
is good and the service is friendly yet cor-
rect. *(Also see Londra Palace hotel entry).*
Choose a seat on the terrace to watch the
world go by. Alternatively, just have a drink
at the cosy bar inside. Best to reserve but
not always necessary.

Harry's Bar
Calle Vallaresso
San Marco 1323
Tel: 041-5285777
Open daily, 10am–11pm.
A well-known Venetian institution, run by
Harry (Arrigo) Cipriani and full of people
trying to spot celebrities. The cuisine is still

considered the best in Venice, particularly
pasta. *Carpaccio* is the speciality which
Hemingway used to enjoy here. It is considered more chic to eat in the simpler down-
stairs bar.

Harry's Dolci
Fondamenta San Biagio
Giudecca 773
(close to Sant'Eufemia landing stage)
Tel: 041-5224844/5208337
San Marco vaporetto stop.
*Closed Tuesday and November to mid-
March.*
Offshoot of Harry's Bar with similar food
at slightly cheaper prices and excellent cakes
served all day. Outdoor terrace with views
over the Giudecca Canal. Chic clientele.

La Cusina
Hotel Europa e Regina
Calle Larga XXII Marzo
San Marco 2161
Tel: 041-5200477
*San Marco or Santa Maria del Giglio va-
poretto stops.*
Superb standards. Discreet atmosphere;
summer terrace.

Locanda Cipriani
Torcello
Tel: 041-730150
Fax: 041-735433
*Open for lunch and dinner, except on Tues-
day. Closed in winter.*
Set on the remote but lovely island of Torcello, this is a gentrified yet rustic spot serv-
ing simpler cuisine than in the other Cipriani
establishments (notably at the two Harry's).
Despite the air of rusticity, prices are relatively high but ingredients are fresh, dishes
refined and service personalised. Best to
book, and try to visit slightly out of season,
when it has more atmosphere.

Moderate Restaurants
L60,000–120,000
Compared with other big cities, most restaurants close early in Venice, around 10.30pm,
with last orders often well before 10pm. This
is true of both expensive and moderately
priced restaurants. Inexpensive restaurants
have more varied opening times.

Agli Alboretti
Rio Terrà Marco Foscarini
Dorsoduro 882
Tel: 041-5230058
Closed Wednesday all day and Thursday
lunchtime.
Charming, yet upmarket trattoria that spills
onto a leafy courtyard. A popular place
which excels at creative interpretations of
traditional Venetian cuisine.

Ai Assassini
Rio Terrà dei Assassini
Sant'Angelo
San Marco 3695
Tel: 041-5287986
Sant'Angelo vaporetto stop.
Open 11.30am–3pm, 6.45–11pm. Closed
Sunday.
Set close to the doomed site of the Fenice
opera house, this gentrified inn offers a wide
range of dishes from a regularly changing
menu. Highlights include the wide range of
Venetian and classic Italian starters. In the
evening, the restaurant draws a young crowd.

Ai Cugnai
Piscina del Forner
Dorsoduro 857
Tel: 041-5289238
Closed Monday and January.
Busy trattoria run by three sisters, just two
minutes from the Accademia. Small, old-
fashioned and homely with wood-panelling
and pictures.

Al Conte Pescaor
Piscina San Zulian
San Marco 544
Tel: 041-5221483
Closed Sunday in winter.
A small and authentic fish restaurant with an
old-fashioned air and warm atmosphere, sit-
uated close to San Marco; attracts a local
trade as well as being popular with visitors.

Alla Madonna
(Rialto area)
San Polo 594
Tel: 041-5223824
San Silvestro vaporetto stop.
Open for lunch and dinner daily (until
10.30pm), except on Wednesday.
A classic, reasonably priced Venetian *trat-*
toria with a wide choice. Given its closeness
to the Rialto fish market, seafood is natu-
rally the mainstay, including such dishes as
fried eel or spaghetti with cuttlefish.

Al Mascaròn
Calle Lunga Santa Maria Formosa
Castello 5525
Tel: 041-5225995
Rialto or San Zaccaria vaporetto stops.
Open 11am–3pm, 7.30pm–midnight. Closed
Sunday.
This is one of the most popular inns in Venice,
so it's best to reserve. The convivial atmo-
sphere is bustling and fun. Typical dishes
include fresh seafood, such as spaghetti with
mussels or cuttlefish.

Above: restaurant at the Rialto Bridge

Al Ponte del Diavolo
Torcello 10
Tel: 041-730401
Closed Wednesday.
Al Ponte del Diavolo is an appealing inn, offering excellent pasta and seafood, delivered with professional service. Also has a good ambience. Makes an ideal lunch venue in Torcello.

Antica Bessetta
Salizzada Ca' Zusto
Santa Croce 1395
(near San Giacomo dell'Orio)
Tel: 041-721687
Riva de Biasio vaporetto stop.
Closed Tuesday, also Wednesday morning.
This restaurant can be difficult to find but is well worth the effor. If offers a relaxed, casual atmosphere and authentic food. It is a popular choice of chefs.

Antica Sacrestia
Calle Sacrestia
Castello 4442
Tel: 041-5230749
San Zaccaria vaporetto stop.
Closed Monday.
This is an old-fashioned trattoria situated off Campo Santi Filippo e Giacomo. Its menu includes sound fish, a number of Venetian specialities, good pizzas and a vegetarian menu.

Corte Sconta
Calle del Pestrin
Castello 3886
Tel: 041-5227024
Arsenale or Tana vaporetto stop.
Closed Sunday and Monday.
An inviting seafood restaurant located close to the Arsenal. Authentic Venetian dishes. Popular with locals and visitors alike.

Trattoria da Fiore
Calle delle Botteghe
(off Campo Santo Stefano)
San Marco 3461
Tel: 041-5235310
San Samuele or Sant'Angelo vaporetto stops.
Open 11.30am–4pm, 6pm–midnight. Closed Tuesday.
Set close to Campo Santo Stefano and *Palazzo* Grassi, this traditional bar and inn is usually popular for its excellent *cicchetti* (local tapas), served at extremely reasonable prices. Although the prices are lower if you eat at the bar, the menu is also more restricted. The adjoining cosy restaurant is also well worth trying for its wide selection of traditional Venetian dishes, including *spaghetti al cartoccio* and *fritto misto* (mixed fried fish).

Trattoria da Remigio
Salizzada dei Greci
Castello 3416
Tel: 041-5230089
Closed Monday and Tuesday.
Excellent, if pricey, fish and seafood. A large, bustling trattoria. Book ahead.

Trattoria da Romano
Via B Galuppi, 221
Island of Burano
Tel: 041-730030
Set on the colourful island of Burano, this is a popular, artistic *trattoria* that has welcomed numerous celebrities over the years. They have professed to being charmed by the artistic atmosphere, casual welcome and the straightforward cuisine. The place, overlooking the sea, has long been a favourite with artists, who enjoy the seafood and marine views as much as anyone else. Catch *motonave* number 12 back to central Venice.

Left: café near the Ponte dell'Accademia

eating out

Vini da Gigio
Fondamenta San Felice
Cannaregio 328
Tel: 041-528 5140
Open daily, except Monday.
This cosy, atmospheric inn enjoys a canalside setting and good food. Children welcome.

Inexpensive Restaurants
L30,000–60,000
If you are happy with more informal dining, there are an increasing number of places that offer drinks, substantial Venetian snacks, even simple full meals. In fact, such inns and bars are often a lot more representative of what passes for authentic Venetian dining than many restaurants. Some of these places are open for lunch and dinner while others have more of a reputation as nightspots *(see Nightlife, page 72)*.

Alla Rivetta
Ponte San Provolo
Castello 4625
Tel: 041-5287302
Closed Monday, July and August.
Cosy if chaotic trattoria. Set behind San Marco, off Campo San Filippo e Giacomo, this popular if rather cramped place offers home cooking and Venetian specialities, served by welcoming staff.

Al Vecio Canton
Castello 4738/a
Tel: 041-5285176
Al Vecio Canton is an authentic and atmospheric pizzeria located between Ruga Giuffa and Campo San Provolo (near Riva degli Schiavoni).

All'Antica Mola
Fondamenta degli Ormesini
Cannaregio, 2800
Tel: 041-717492
Tre Archi vaporetto stop.
Off the beaten track (and set in a converted mill), this trattoria is close to the ghetto. Not as simple as it used to be, it is still a good place to dine with the locals and try some typical Venetian cuisine. Nothing beats sitting in the garden on a summer's evening and eating a fish grill or the other Venetian specialities on offer.

Pizzerie
Given that many Venetian restaurants represent poor value for money, it makes sense to pop into a pizzeria now and again, both to economise and to enjoy a simple pizza in unstuffy surroundings.

Al Sole di Napoli
Campo Santa Margherita
Dorsoduro 3023
Tel: 041-528 5686
Ca' Rezzonico vaporetto stop.
Open daily for lunch and dinner.
Despite new management, Al Sole di Napoli remains a popular *pizzeria*, with the bonus of outdoor tables for summer dining. It is situated on one of the liveliest squares in Dorsoduro so you should expect to wait a little while for a table.

Bora Bora
Calle dei Stagneri
Campo San Bartolomeo
San Marco 5251
Tel: 041-5236583
Rialto vaporetto stop.
Open daily, for lunch and dinner.
Bora Bora is a small but reliable *pizzeria* situated in the heart of the bustling Rialto area. Service is speedy, with a take-away service available.

La Perla
Rio Terra dei Franceschi
Santi Apostoli
Cannaregio 4615
Tel: 041-5285175
Ca d'Oro or Rialto vaporetto stop.
Open daily, except Monday.
This popular pizzeria has more than 90 different pizzas on its menu. Expect to wait for a table at weekends.

Ethnic Restaurants
La Perla d'Oriente
Campo dei Frari
San Polo 3004
Tel: 041-5237229
San Toma vaporetto stop.
Open daily, until midnight.
This fairly elegant Chinese restaurant is popular with Venetians and foreigners alike. Prices are moderate.

Le Notti d'Oriente

Fondamenta della Misericordia
Cannareggio 2578
Tel: 041-717315
Sant'Alvise or San Marcuola vaporetto stops.
Open daily until 11.30pm.
Set in the heart of Cannareggio, where most ethnic restaurants are found, this is an affordable, contemporary-looking Middle-Eastern restaurant. Lebanese and Jordanian specialities include *mezze* (such as falafel and hummous), as well as grilled meats.

Rustic Inns and Wine Bars ('Bacari')

In terms of price, these places range from inexpensive to extremely cheap, depending whether you have tapas-style snacks or a full meal. Unlike classic restaurants and *trattorie*, inns (known as *osterie*) and *bacari* (Venetian wine bars and tapas bars) are open at unusual times, with many tending to open or close quite early. Several *bacari*, especially the ones near the Rialto fish market, are rough and ready, while others are simple yet cosy rustic inns. It is unheard of to book, but you could call before setting out, in case opening hours have changed.

Ae Do Spade

Calle delle Do Spade
Rialto
San Polo 860
Tel: 041-5210574
San Silvestro vaporetto stop.
Open 9am–3pm, and 5–11pm. Closed Sunday, except in summer
At first sight, it seems highly touristy, but this inn is, in fact, popular with Venetians. The signature dish is the spicy sandwich known as *paperini*. Prompt and friendly service.

Al Milion

Corte al Milion
Cannareggio 5841
Tel: 041-5229302
Closed Sunday and August.
An old wine tavern offering a large range of snacks and seafood. Be prepared to queue. It's hidden behind the church of San Giovanni (near the Rialto) in a courtyard where Marco Polo's house allegedly stood. Recommended are the *pasta e fagioli*, fish soup or *carpaccio*.

Al Volto

Calle Cavalli
San Luca
San Marco 4081
Tel: 041-5228945
Rialto vaporetto stop.
Open 10am–2.30pm, 5–10.30pm. Closed Sunday.
This historic wine bar lies in a side street close to the Rialto. The atmospheric interior is lined with wine bottles; a reflection of the vast choice on offer. Wine-tastings are accompanied by nibbles on simple but good *cicchetti, Venetian tapas* snacks.

Antico Dolo

Ruga Vecchia San Giovanni
(Close to the Rialto Bridge)
San Polo 778
Tel: 041-5226546
San Silvestro vaporetto stop.
Open 10am–3pm, 6.30–10pm. Closed Sunday.
This Venetian tapas bar serves excellent *bruschette* topped with grilled vegetables or with Venetian stockfish *(mantecato)*. The menu is fairly limited but reliable and cheap.

Da Pinto

Campo delle Beccarie
(Close to Rialto market)
San Polo 367
Tel: 041-5224599
San Silvestro vaporetto stop.
Open 7.30am–7pm. Closed Monday.
This is the rustic spot Venetians call into while going about their food shopping in

the Rialto market. Among the typical tasty snacks usually available are *baccala mantecato, salami, mortadella* and *bruschetta*, all accompanied by simple Veneto wines sold by the glass.

Do Mori
Calle Dei Do Mori
(off Ruga Vecchia San Giovanni)
San Polo 429
Tel: 041-5225401
San Silvestro vaporetto stop.
Open 9am–1pm, 5–8pm. Closed all day Sunday and Wednesday afternoon.
Authentic, rough and ready Rialto bar with good selection of wines.

Vino Vino
Ponte delle Veste
San Marco 2007a
Tel: 041-5237027
Open 11am–midnight, closed Tuesday.
Large selection of Italian (and other) wines served by the glass or bottle. Also rustic-style Venetian dishes.

Historic Cafés, Cake Shops and Snacks

Venice abounds in traditional places for savoury and inexpensive snacks. (These are essentially covered in *Rustic Inns and Wine Bars* above). However, there are a number of traditional cafés which are popular at all times of day. The grand atmosphere and setting, with an orchestra playing on Piazza San Marco, more than justifies the high prices charged. Even Venetians are happy to indulge themselves in such places from time to time.

To avoid service charge (exorbitant if you are sitting out on a terrace), stand at a bar or café for *panini* (bread rolls with fillings), *tramezzini* (fat sandwiches, often with delicious fillings) or *cicchetti* – savoury snacks, such as meat balls, baby squid, artichoke hearts, cheese or *prosciutto*, usually taken with wine. If you are feeling adventurous try *nervetti*, ox nerves boiled with onions, pepper and salt, then cut into small pieces. There are several self-service places with tables. *Pizzerias* can be surprisingly expensive by the time the cover charge and service charge have been added.

Right: historic Caffè Florian's gilded interior

Venice has no shortage of excellent cafés. The most elegant is undoubtedly Florian's in Piazza San Marco; it has been a meeting place for Venetian society since 1720. Here a simple *cappuccino* costs around L12,000; a salmon sandwich, which is only another L6,000, seems cheap by comparison. If the orchestra is playing you should add another L8,000 to your order.

The larger squares of the city have numerous cheaper open-air cafés and there are plenty of bars for taking a pre-prandial *ombra* or glass of wine. *Pasticcerie* throughout the city have tempting cakes, croissants, pastries and strudel – a legacy of the Austrian occupation.

Piazza San Marco Cafés:
Florian's: this is the most famous of the grand Venetian cafés, complete with its own orchestra.
Quadri: another legendary spot, also with its own orchestra.
Lavena: supposedly serves the best coffee in Venice.

Marchini
Ponte San Maurizio
(Off Campo Santo Stefano)
Santa Maria del Giglio vaporetto.
Come here for melt-in-your-mouth pastries, biscuits, chocolates, as well as the odd savoury items, in one of the best *patisccerie* in Venice.

Rosa Salva
Mercerie San Salvador 5020
San Marco
Tel: 041-5227934
Rialto vaporetto stop.
This noted café is set in the bustling Mercerie shopping and commercial district close to San Marco. This is the place for a light but authentically Venetian breakfast of croissant, coffee and possibly a pastry. However, the café offers tempting treats at all times of day, both sweet and savoury.

Ice Cream Parlours

Venice has a number of good ice cream parlours, with the best of them situated on the Zattere, the airy promenade that provides a pleasant diversion in the stultifying summer heat. The most famous Venetian ice cream is *gianduiotti con panna,* chocolate ice cream generally served in a glass with frozen cream.

Da Nico (Zattere, Dorsoduro 922 Zattere *vaporetto* stop)
Al Cucciolo (Zattere, Dorsoduro 782, Zattere *vaporetto* stop)
Causin (Campo Santa Margherita, Dorsoduro 2996, Ca' Rezzonico *vaporetto* stop)
Paolin (café and ice cream parlour, Campo Santo Stefano, Dorsoduro)

Apart from some excellent ice cream parlours, Dorsoduro has a varied range of bars and restaurants, many of them with pleasant gardens, so it is worth heading to the area simply to eat and drink . There are quite a few authentic and atmospheric *trattorie* providing genuine Venetian cuisine, but these are booked very quickly as Dorsoduro is such a popular area. It also has the greatest concentration of atmospheric open-air bars in Venice.

NIGHTLIFE

No one comes to Venice for nightclubs, which don't really exist. As for discotheques, most young Venetians go to Lido di Jesolo, at least in the summer, and return by car, somewhat the worse for wear, in the morning. Instead, traditional city nightlife revolves around cosy bars, and low-key live music. Most of the bars listed below are inexpensive, particularly those that just serve *cicchetti* (Venetian tapas). For young people, Campo Santa Margherita in Dorsoduro is the centre for what passes as city nightlife. However, there are also a number of trendy and faintly alternative pubs and clubs in the Cannareggio district. (Given the conservative nature of the city and the shortage of young Venetians who live in the centre, genuinely alternative pubs and clubs are rare).

More sophisticated nightlife is aimed at an older, moneyed crowd and is generally restricted to the bars and piano bars in and around the grand hotels, such as the Danieli, Cipriani, Gritti, Luna Baglioni and Londra Palace *(see relevant entries in Hotels).* These hotels are perfectly happy accepting non-residents in their elegant, yet often slightly soulless, bars and restaurants. For elegance, and possibly romance, the tinkling pianos, waterside terraces and sweeping rooftop restaurants of the grand hotels fit the bill. Something to do at least once is to visit Venice Casino, set in the gorgeous Renaissance Palazzo Vendramin Calergi on the Grand Canal (Tel: 041-5297111; open until 2.30am in winter only; San Marcuola *vaporetto* stop).

However, for atmosphere and a truer sense of the city, the intimate Venetian bars are more fun. Recently, normally sedate Venetian nightlife has been shaken up by the opening of lively pubs, some of which offer live music. *Al Paradiso Perduto (see below)* is typical of this new wave of bars.

All'Arco
Calle dell'Ochialer, Rialto
San Polo 436
Tel: 041-5205666
San Silvestro vaporetto stop.
Open 7.30am–3pm, 6.30–10pm. Closed Sunday.
This small inn is the popular haunt of young

Left: sunset on the lagoon

Venetians in search of pre-dinner drinks and snacks. At 7pm, join the crowd in munching *cicchetti* (Venetian tapas) and sipping a glass of sparkling, dry Prosecco wine.

All'Ombra
Campiello Flaminio Correr
San Giovanni Grisostomo
Cannareggio 5603
Tel: 041-5208524
Rialto vaporetto stop.
Open 8am–3pm, 6.30pm–1am. Closed Monday.
This popular new inn, set on a lively little square, attracts both visitors and young Venetians in search of a late-night meeting-place in permanently sleepy Venice.

Al Paradiso Perduto
Fondamenta della Misericordia
Cannareggio 2540
Tel: 041-720581
San Marcuola vaporetto stop.
Open Monday to Saturday 7pm–2am; Sunday 11am–3pm, 7pm–2am. Closed Wednesday.
This is a large, boisterous bar and inn which attracts a trendy, arty young crowd, representative of the 'new' Venetian nightlife. There is always background or live music, accompanied by typical hearty Venetian fare.

Margaret du Champ
Campo Santa Margherita
Dorsoduro 3019
Tel: 041-5286255
Set in the liveliest square in Dorsoduro, this fashionable bar is pleasant throughout the day, but particularly lively in the evening.

Round Midnight
Ponte dei Pugni
Dorsoduro 3102
Tel: 041-5232056
Unusually for Venice, this is a disco-bar where one can dance. The club, a hot-spot in the 1980s, has recently been revamped.

The Fiddler's Elbow
Strada Nuova
Cannareggio 3847
Tel: 041-5239930
Set in the main shopping street in the Cannareggio quarter, this is a popular, if pretty fake, traditional Irish pub which attracts a young international crowd.

Vino Vino
Calle del Cafetier
(by Ponte delle Veste)
San Fantin
San Marco 2007/a
Tel: 041-5237027
Santa Maria del Giglio vaporetto stop.
Open daily 10.30am–midnight; until 1am on Saturday.
This small wine bar and restaurant serves Venetian tapas and a wide selection of Italian and foreign wines.

Romantic Gondola Rides
The most pleasurable evening pursuit in Venice is to take to the canals in a gondola. This symbol of the city has been carrying passengers and cargo for more than 1,000 years. By the 16th century there were around 10,000 gondolas operating here – now there are a mere 400. For grace and elegance there is nothing to rival the gondola. It is sleek and black, elegantly curved at either end and manoeuvred by a single oar. The gondolier stands at the rear, rowing and steering the boat with amazing dexterity.

The 16th-century gondola was a brightly coloured, richly carved vessel and nobles used to vie with each other over the number they owned and the ornamentation their boats displayed. But sumptuary decrees in the 17th century forbade any sort of ostentation. All boats were to be painted black and the *felze*, the cabins providing passengers' anonymity and protection from the rain, were to be stripped of their lavish coverings. Only foreign ambassadors were exempt from the law. Since then gondolas have been painted black – prompting allusions to mystery, melancholia and death. The vast majority of today's gondolas are only used by visitors. Wealthy Venetians own a motor launch, which is faster and cheaper to maintain.

Although charges are regulated, gondoliers are notorious for cheating tourists, so make sure you agree a fee before you setting off – 50 minutes should cost in the region of L150,000. Booking as a group convoy may work out cheaper, although there is a maximum limit of 6 people per boat.

CALENDAR OF EVENTS

The only off-peak season in Venice is mid-winter when low temperatures, grey skies and the risk of flooding put off tourists. Wintry mists have romantic appeal but it can be just plain cold and foggy. Springtime can be surprisingly cool and there is no real guarantee of warm sunshine until May. The best months overall to be in Venice are May, June, September and October. The most crowded times are Carnival, Easter and mid-summer.

Although many of Venice's traditional festivals have fixed dates, the city is also home to an ever-changing series of cultural events. The National Call Centre is a direct number for information on events, shows and exhibitions. The operators speak English, French, German and Spanish, as well as Italian. If calling from Italy, it is a freephone number: 800-117700 (open 8am–11pm). However, if calling from abroad, the call is chargeable: 0039-06-419007.

January–March

The advantages of visiting between January and March are cheaper hotel prices and fewer tourists (Carnival aside). Duckboards and gumboots come out when the signs go up or the sirens are sounded for the *acque alte*, high waters. This is a good time of year for opera lovers (season – November to May).

New Year on the beach: it is a long-standing tradition for Venetians to meet their friends and family on the beach to wish one another Happy New Year. Many bring food and wine, or attend an organised beach party.

The winter peace is briefly disturbed by the **Carnival** two weeks before Lent. The 18th century was the great age of masked balls and carnivals, but all this came to an abrupt halt when the republic fell and Napoleon had all the masks burnt. Carnival was only revived in the late 1970s. It lasts for 10 days, during which time masks are donned, fantasies and passions acted out, and social divisions discarded. The whole city becomes a stage set for exotic costumes, pageants and concerts, culminating on Shrove Tuesday with a huge masked ball in the Piazza and a firework display over the Bacino di San Marco. Anyone wanting a room should book several months ahead.

Masks and costumes can be hired in Venice. **Su e Zo per I Ponti**, held on the Sunday that falls in the middle of March, is a lively mini-marathon through the alleys of the city.

April

April sees the arrival of the package tourists. Temperatures can be surprisingly low and there is a risk of rain.

St Mark's Day (25th), is when the gondoliers hold a race between Sant'Elena and the Punta della Dogana and traditionally everyone eats *risi e bisi* (rice and peas).

May

Spring is a good time for concerts at the Palafenice and in city churches. Favourite event of the season is the **Vogalonga**, held on the Sunday after Ascension Day, La Sensa. The word literally means 'long row' and the event involves hundreds of rowing boats following a course to Burano and back – about 32km (20 miles). Anyone with an oar-powered craft is welcome to take part. The race has its origins in the days when the doge would row out to the Lido in his ornate *Bucintoro* (state barge) and ceremonially cast a ring into the water, symbolising the marriage of Venice to the sea.

June

In odd-numbered years, June sees the start of the **Biennale Contemporary Art Exhibition**. It is held in permanent pavilions in the public gardens and lasts until September. Exhibitions are also held at numerous city venues, such as churches and the salt and rope warehouses. The centenary of the Biennale was celebrated in 1995.

The Biennale is expanding with every edition, and occupying an increasingly wide range of buildings in the historic districts, as well as all the standard venues in the Giardini (public gardens) and the pavilions. The city also uses the occasion as the centrepoint of a series of exhibitions and events in different fields, from concerts to debates and general festivities. The millennium edition of the Biennale saw the opening of exhibitions in 61 sites, from inns, churches, Gothic palaces and libraries to old tea warehouses and a former rope factory. In terms of promotion and funding, the Biennale is now a major event. In the city's American pavilion, for instance, $1.5 million of Gucci funding sponsored an artist to sprinkle vermilion paint around the site; the paint was so toxic that, it had to be vacuumed away by cleaners wearing respirators every night. (For details of the Biennale, check the dedicated website: www.labiennale.org. or call the Biennale organisation on: 041-5226514).

July–September

These are the months to avoid, when the city is hot and crowded. Main event is the **Festa del Redentore** (July, 3rd weekend), when a bridge of boats is built across the Giudecca Canal to the Redentore – the church which was built in gratitude for deliverance of the city from the plague of 1576. The festival is a colourful event with hundreds of people rowing out to picnic on the water. It ends with fireworks and crowds rowing out to the Lido to watch the sun rise.

Assumption: at Ferragosto, 15 August, the Assumption is celebrated in a classical concert in the cathedral on the island of Torcello.

Late August/early September is celebrity-spotting time on the Lido, as the **International Film Festival** takes place here for two weeks. As far as American and European movie stars are concerned, the Venice Film Festival is a high point on the international calendar. Although the Palazzo del Cinema on the Lido is the main focus for the film previews, the celebrity effect causes ripples throughout the city, from the grand hotels to the most intimate bars.

On the first Sunday in September the **Regata Storica** (historical regatta) opens with a spectacular procession of traditional boats on the Grand Canal, with rowers in costume. During the days of the Serene Republic, these historic regattas celebrated anything from the election of a new Doge to the arrival of a foreign prince.

On 11–12 September, the city hosts an appealing **antiques fair** on Campo San Maurizio, with silverware and jewellery for sale.

November–December

Autumn tends to be the time of some of the biggest artistic events, with such venues as the Fiat-run **Palazzo Grassi** staging grandiose international exhibitions. Recent

shows have been dedicated to major artists or to an entire civilisation such as the Phoenicians or the Etruscans. (For details on shows at the Palazzo Grassi, call: 041-5231680).In autumn, the ballet, classical music and operatic seasons are also underway, with events staged in the Teatro Goldoni and at the PalaFenice. The company known as the Gran Teatro La Fenice has been performing there since the devastating fire that burnt down the opera house in 1996. The legendary **La Fenice** opera house is unfortunately still closed at present. Although the city insists that it will be rebuilt within the next few years, those in the know believe that it will take at least five years. In the meantime, performances take place in the tented **PalaFenice**. For opera tickets call the box office on 041-5210161/0141-786562. Or check the following website: www.tin.it/fenice. Email: fenice @bigliettoelettronico.it.

Cultural Venice: websites

The following are useful sources of information to some of the city's major events:

Venice Carnival (Carnevale di Venezia): www.venicecarnival.iti.it/
Palazzo Grassi: www.palazzograssi.it/ (Guide to exhibitions in this grand venue)
La Fenice opera house: www.cosi.it/fenice/
Venice tourist office (APT Venezia): www.provincia.venezia.it/aptve/

Right: dress for the occasion

MONEY MATTERS

The basic unit of currency is the lira (L). Coins come in denominations of 50, 100, 200 and 500 lire; banknotes come in denominations of 1,000, 2,000, 5,000, 10,000, 20,000, 50,000 and 100,000 lire.

Bank hours vary but are generally Monday to Friday 8.30am–1.30pm and 3–4pm; most have Bancomat cash dispensers outside. The bank at the railway station is open weekdays from 8am–5.30pm. The American Express office (Salizzada San Moisè) is open 8am–8pm in summer.

Traveller's Cheques are one of the safest ways of carrying money. Lost or stolen American Express cheques can usually be replaced within 24 hours.

Tipping

In restaurants service is normally included but it is usual to leave a little extra if you think the waiter or waitress deserves it. Hotel bills always include service but tip the porter for carrying your bags. Custodians in churches who light paintings or pinpoint masterpieces for you will appreciate a tip – or at least something for the church.

GETTING AROUND

Venice is surprisingly small. Going from north to south on foot takes only half an hour – if you happen to know the city well. First-time visitors always get lost. The most

comprehensive, accurate (and expensive) map is the *Touring Club Italia*, not easily found outside Italy. The map contained in the back of this guide traces the routes described in the Day and Pick & Mix itineraries, but should also help you to explore the city independently.

If you do manage to get lost, remember you are unlikely to be far from the invaluable yellow signs which point the way to major landmarks: San Marco, Rialto, Ferrovia (railway station) and Piazzale Roma (bus station). The Grand Canal, sweeping through the heart of the city, provides another vital landmark

Waterbuses *(Vaporetti)*

Although you will probably spend most of your time exploring the city on foot, the main form of public transport is the *vaporetto* or water bus. The routes and times are subject to change so if staying more than a few days, it is best to call in at the ACTV water transport offices on Piazzale Roma (tel: 041-5287886), or consult the ACTV website: www.actv.it/inglese. The tourist offices do not supply public transport maps). Given the costs of maintaining Venice, and the difficulties of protecting this unique environment, there are plans afoot to dramatically increase the cost of water transport, and to introduce a high fare for travelling on the Grand Canal, in particular. (Residents already benefit from subsidised public transport).

The waterbus network is excellent, providing reasonably priced trips through and around the city. Best value is Line 1, the so-called *accelerato*, which travels the length of the Grand Canal stopping at every landing stage. Line 82 (red) provides a faster service down the Grand Canal making only six stops. It goes west as far as Tronchetto (the car park island) and east along the Giudecca Canal to San Zaccaria (and the Lido in summer). Line 52, the *Circolare* (and the fast route between the station and San Marco), skirts the periphery of Venice in both directions and takes in the Lido. Some of the ferry routes have changed recently, including the 51 and 52. This circular route no longer serves the Arsenal area, or passes through the historic boatyards. The circular line, No. 52, provides an enjoyable ride

Left: gondola booking system

around the periphery of Venice and takes in the island of Murano. Lines 51 and 52 are still a circular route but the route now goes up the Cannareggio Canal before skirting the shores of Northern Venice, and eventually reaching the Lido.

Lines 41 and 42 now provide the only route through the mysterious Arsenal and boatyard area. These lines represent a circular route through both outer and inner Venice. Other boats (Lines 6, 12, 14, 61, 62) provide a service to the Lido and islands.

The system is simple to follow provided you have a map with the updated waterbus routes (they change frequently). Note the destinations signed on landing stages (particularly those at the busy termini of the Ferrovia, San Zaccaria and Fondamente Nuove), to ensure you are going in the right direction. If you are unsure, ask the crew member who helps passengers on and off the boat.

Tickets are available from most landing stages, some bars, tobacconists and shops displaying the ACTV sign. For the one ticket you can stay on the boat for as long as you like. Children under 1m (3ft) tall go free, but a suitcase costs as much as an ordinary passenger. A single ticket costs L6,000 and must be stamped before boarding. A carnet of ten one-way tickets costs 50,000 lire, and can be used over a period of time. A ticket entitling you to unlimited journeys for 24 hours on lines is available (L18,000), as is a three-day ticket (L35,000) and a weekly ticket (L60,000), as well as group and family tickets. Information on the waterbus system and a current route map are available from the ACTV offices in Piazzale Roma

Gondolas

Gondoliers may take you for a ride in both senses of the word *(see Nightlife)* so check the tariff and agree the fare. Ask at any travel agent for information on serenaded gondola 'groups'. The cheapest gondola is the *traghetto*, a ferry crossing the Grand Canal in six different places. A return ticket on a *traghetto* costs 5,000 lire, and allows for two trips which must be made on the same day.

Water Taxis

These smart, varnished launches take up to four people. All of them have meters and must display a list of charges (from L40,000) and a map of the city. You can find taxi 'ranks' at main points in the city, otherwise call 041-5235775 or 041-5222303. To understand the complex system of charges for water transport, pick up a copy of *Meeting in Venice* from a tourist office or news kiosk.

Addresses

If you don't know the system, finding an address in Venice can be extremely tricky. Buildings are numbered not by the streets but by the administrative areas of the city. For example in the *Sestiere* of San Marco, the numbering starts with the Doge's Palace (No 1), works its way round the quarter and ends up at the Rialto. The address is simply the *sestiere* and the number, eg Castello 3348. If you are taking note of an address in Venice ask for a landmark (a church or street name) to help you get there.

Many streets, squares or churches are written in different ways, sometimes in Italian, sometimes in Venetian dialect. A name marked on a street or square may not always correspond to that given on a map or in the itineraries. Note the following before you start exploring the city.

calle	street
campo	square
campiello	small square
rio	canal
fondamenta	street along a canal
salizzada	paved street
ponte	bridge
sottoportico/	
sottoportego	covered passageway
corte, cortile	courtyard

COMMUNICATIONS

The main Post Office (open Monday to Saturday, 8.30am–7pm), located close to the Rialto Bridge in the Fondaco dei Tedeschi, is worth visiting simply to see its fine courtyard. You can also send telegrams and faxes from here.

Stamps can be bought in bars and tobacconists displaying a white 'T'. The main post office provides a fax, telegram and telephone service for all destinations. Telephone cards

can be purchased from post offices and most tobacconists *(tabacchi)*. To use the card, break off the marked corner and then insert, arrow first.

Public telephones take phone cards *(schede telefoniche)*. To call a Venice number from anywhere in Italy (and from within Venice), use the 041- prefix.

To dial other countries first dial the international access code 00, then the relevant country code as follows: Australia (61); France (33); Germany (49); Japan (81); Netherlands (31); Spain (34); UK (44); US and Canada (1). If you are using a US credit phone card, dial the company's access number as given below – Sprint, tel: 172 1877; AT&T, tel: 172 1011; MCI, tel: 172 1022.

HEALTH & EMERGENCIES

Venice is one of the safest cities in Europe but you should watch your valuables in crowded places, especially on the *vaporetti*, the inter-island boats. It is best to leave valuables in the hotel safe and carry money on you rather than in a shoulder bag or handbag.

If you are unfortunate enough to be robbed, head straight to the police *(Questura)* to make an official declaration. A lost passport should be reported to your consulate.

General Emergency
Tel: 113/112

Police
Fondamenta San Lorenzo,
Castello 5053
Tel: 041-2715772; 112 (emergency)

Fire Brigade
Tel: 115/041-5200222

Hospitals
A 24-hour casualty department operates at Ospedale Civile, Campo Santi Giovanni e Paolo, Tel: 041-5294588/5230000.

Pharmacies
Local newspapers and the booklet *Un Ospite di Venezia* (available from big hotels) list late-night pharmacies. A late-night rota is also posted on all pharmacy doors. Also get the *Venice Pocket* booklet from the tourist office.

ACCOMMODATION

Where to stay
Unless booking with a reputable operator or relying on a personal recommendation, accommodation in Venice is a minefield. Most itineraries assume you are staying within easy reach of San Marco, where many of the hotels are concentrated. As a general rule, the closer you are to San Marco, the higher the price, but there are many exceptions, with several pricey hotels on the Lido and Giudecca, for instance. For families with young children, the Lido makes a good choice, with its sandy beaches and bike rides. Although not the bargain it once was, the romantic Dorsoduro district, about ten minutes walk from San Marco, is a charming area to stay, and has smaller but still relatively expensive hotels. The cheaper alternative is the station area, which is not nearly as attractive, but convenient if you are arriving by train or car and only staying a night or two. The far reaches of the Castello district are generally an appealing option for historic but less pricey hotels (see *La Residenza* entry below).

If forced to stay outside central Venice, avoid depressing Mestre on the mainland, and only stay in the garish beach resort of Lido di Jesolo if you want lively young nightlife or must have a beach. It is better to stay a 30-minute train ride from Venice and make forays into the city. Among the best options is the historic university city of Padua, not to mention Treviso, the same distance away, which has an old quarter similar to Venice. (The latter is particularly convenient given that low-cost carriers such as Ryanair now fly from the UK to Treviso).

Above: foreign correspondence

practical information

When to Visit
Since there is almost no off-season in Venice, only a small blip in late January, hotels can easily be fully booked all-year-round. Unfortunately, this means that hoteliers can afford to try less hard to keep the clientele happy and eager to return. In any case, make reservations ahead of peak seasons such as Carnival (February), Easter and summer (June to September, until the end of the Venice Film Festival). If making a **last-minute booking**, the official Association of Venetian Hoteliers *(details below)* is your best bet. But if central Venice is full, check exactly where and what is being proposed, and the public transport: the difference, for similar prices, can be a restored *palazzo* in Dolo or an anonymous modern hotel in Mestre. (Although the Association is honourable, you still need to ask the questions).

Cost and Quality
Hotels in Venice are notoriously expensive, with a simple, central hotel here often the same price as a three-star hotel elsewhere in Italy. In addition, the unique location and environmental circumstances mean that Venice hotel prices can be about 30 per cent higher than on the mainland. And Venetian breakfasts can easily be 30 per cent less good than on the mainland, even in top hotels. Also check if VAT (TVA) and breakfast are included in the quote. Prices can be lower out of season but to discover these, it is best to contact the hotel directly and try some gentle bargaining. Certainly, there are positive exceptions but, even so, it is a seller's market. The basic rules in Venice are: book early, and check where your room faces, and what the price differential is between "good" rooms and "bad" rooms. For instance, the same hotel can offer a choice between an expensive large room overlooking the Grand Canal, and a pokey back room overlooking a bleak inner courtyard. Unsuspecting guests in all but the best hotels can all too easily be fobbed off with a dingy broom-cupboard lacking effective central heating and a fully-functional shower. It pays to shop around. For any **complaints** on accommodation or other matters, call the freephone number (in Italy): 800-355 920, which puts you in touch with a department of the local tourist board.

Directions
When booking a hotel, be Venetian. Don't just request its official address, which can be singularly unhelpful in actually finding the hotel. Instead, ask which is the nearest square/church and ferry stop.

Apartments
Given the costs and variable quality of many Venetian hotels, apartments, particularly for a family or small group, can represent not just a more charming option, but also excellent value for money. This is particularly true in that one can eat at home, one of the greatest pleasures of apartment-living in Venice. Occupying a glorious Gothic *palazzo* also seems to make the world shrink to the old-fashioned wine shop, cheese shop and fish market closest to your temporary home. This is a delightful way to experience the intimacy of Venice, and the pleasures of feeling part of a tightly-knit neighbourhood that feels light years away from the tourist bustle of Carnival masks and gaudy Murano glass. It is extremely difficult to book an apartment from within Venice itself since most of the owners are linked to specific foreign agents or tour operators. Try to book well in advance to secure a good choice.

Venetian Apartments
Tel: 020-8878 1130
Fax: 020-8878 0982
Website: www.venice-rentals.com
This London-based company are the market leaders for Venice, and have a wide selection of highly individualistic apartments, equivalent in price to a reasonably good (but not exorbitant) Venetian hotel. Apartments range from a bijou residence under the eaves to a spacious palace with fabulous views over the Grand Canal. The apartments, which must

Right: Carabinieri patrol the waters

cilious than in other Venetian top hotels. It is worth paying a premium for rooms at the front that overlook the waterside.

Luna Baglioni
Calle Vallaresso
San Marco 1243
Tel: 041-528 9840
Fax: 041-528 7160
Freephone (in Italy): 1678-21057
The Luna's claim to fame is that it is the oldest hotel in Venice, dating back to its foundation in 1118 as a Knights Templar lodge for pilgrims travelling to Jerusalem. Curiously enough, countless restorations and refurbishments mean that the hotel does not really look its age. Conveniently located in the heart of the shopping district, close to Harry's Bar, designer shopping streets, and San Marco itself. The décor is noble Venetian style, but not to everyone's taste: a riot of Murano glass, inlaid marble, and swagged curtains. The hotel boasts an 18th-century ballroom with original ceiling frescoes of courtly scenes and Venetian views. Apart from the impressive restaurant, the Luna also has the grandest breakfast room in Venice.

Metropole
Riva degli Schiavoni
Castello 4149
Tel: 041-520 5044
Fax: 041-522 3679
This four-star hotel is a good and comfortable choice. A patrician residence, it is decorated in grand 19th-century style and has been romantically renovated, and dotted with well-chosen antiques. It is noted for its attentive service, and offers views over courtyards and the Lagoon.

Monaco & Grand Hotel
Calle Vallaresso
San Marco 1325
Tel: 041-5200211
Fax: 041-5200501
Seventy-five rooms. Enjoys an exceptional setting on the Grand Canal with splendid views. This is a hotel of much charm and character which succeeds in feeling more intimate than it is. Gondolas are moored against the sunny terrace. During Venice's notorious high tides and flooding, guests have to walk on raised boards through the reception to reach their rooms, an amusingly surreal experience. This first-rate hotel has improved greatly in recent years. Although comfortable, bedrooms are a little small and sometimes noisy. The best rooms are the ground floor rooms overlooking the Grand Canal. Service and atmosphere are good, however. The entrance is in front of Harry's Bar, universally acknowledged as the most reliable restaurant in Venice.

Saturnia & International
Calle Larga XXII Marzo
San Marco 2398
Tel: 041-5208377
Fax: 041-5207131
Website: www.hotelsaturnia.it
Ninety-five rooms. Occupies an old *palazzo* owned by a family of doges; set on a smart shopping street conveniently close to Piazza San Marco. Has a choice of two restaurants, one of which is open-air. The mood of this distinctive hotel is vaguely medieval in inspiration, which, depending on taste, can be romantic or rather austere. Bedrooms are both intimate and comfortable.

Moderate/Expensive Hotels
Palazzetto Pisani
Canale Grande
Tel: 041-523 2550
Set close to the Accademia Bridge on the Grand Canal, this patrician palace is owned by a direct descendant of Alvise Pisano, who was elected Doge of Venice in 1735. There is a choice of two apartments, one small and one much larger. At the top end of the scale, the most spacious apartment on the *piano nobile* has delightful views over the Grand Canal, and a vast drawing room.

Above: which way to San Marco's?

Moderate Hotels

In general, these are three-star hotels which tend to be smaller and more intimate than the classic grand luxury Venetian affair. Despite their smaller size and relative simplicity, prices are still quite high, ranging from L200,000– 550,000. (The average price for a reasonable double room is approximately L350,000).

Accademia Villa Maravege
Fondamenta Bollani
Dorsoduro 1058–60
Tel: 041-5210188
Fax: 041-5239152
A small, intimate hotel comprising 27 rooms. No longer the bargain it used to be (now L200,000–400,000 for a double), but still very desirable for its quiet location (close to the Accademia), antiques and homely atmosphere. This wisteria-clad hotel is situated in the charming Dorsoduro district at the Grand Canal end of Rio San Trovaso. Reservations should be made months in advance for this corner of old Venice.

Ca' Pisani
Rio Terra Foscarini
Dorsoduro 979a
Tel: 041-277 1478
Fax: 041-277 1061
Set in a historic *palazzo*, this stylish new hotel has shaken up the staid world of Venetian hotels by offering an exceptionally sharp modern design, and rooms at relatively reasonable prices. Although gracing a 14th-century palace near the Accademia, the hotel has a chic Thirties and Forties theme, mixing original and contemporary pieces. All 30 rooms have mini-bars, satellite TV and email facilities, another novelty for Venetian hotels in this category. (Rooms start at around L320,000).

Do Pozzi
Corte dei Due Pozzi
Calle Larga XXII Marzo
San Marco 2373
Tel: 041-5207855
Fax: 041-5229413
Thirty-five rooms. This is a small and spruce hotel situated in quiet cul-de-sac conveniently close to Piazza San Marco.

La Calcina
Zattere
Dorsoduro 780
Tel: 041-5206466
Fax: 041-5227045
Twenty-nine rooms, many looking across to the island of Giudecca. Newly-renovated and appealing, if a touch twee. John Ruskin stayed here.

La Fenice et des Artistes
Campiello della Fenice
San Marco 1936
Tel: 041-5232333
Fax: 041-5203721
Email: fenice@fenicehotels.it
Sixty-five rooms; once popular with performers at the Fenice; good value for Venice, with plenty of charm and character. This individualistic three-star hotel has lost some of its allure with the burning down of La Fenice. Set within a stone's throw of the site of the Fenice (presently closed; rebuilding could take another five years), it is popular with actors, musicians and artists. .

Flora
Calle della Pergola
(Off Larga XXII Marzo)
San Marco 2283a
Tel: 041-5205844
Fax: 041-5228217
Forty-four rooms. One of the most desirable small hotels in Venice with a quiet garden, pretty décor and an excellent location close to Piazza San Marco, this friendly three-star hotel is set in a quiet alley off a prestigious shopping street. Bedrooms vary enormously in size and quality and the single rooms can be quite basic. (Three of the best bedrooms are numbers 45, 46 and 47, which are graced with *fin de siecle* furnishings.) The secluded garden, complete with a Venetian well-head, has recently been remodelled. The courtyard provides a lovely setting for breakfast.

San Cassiano
Calle della Rosa
Santa Croce 2232
Tel: 041-524 1768
Fax: 041-721 033
Email: cassiano@sancassiano'it

stars who flock to the September Venice Film Festival. A four-star hotel with the most character of all those on the Lido, it is located across the road from its private beach. Facilities are similar to those at the Excelsior *(see page 87)* but the hotel is more atmospheric. Large gardens, pool, tennis courts and private cabins – at a price – on the beach. The price of a double room is between L750,000 and L1 million.

Biasutti (Villa Ada)
Via E Dandolo, 27–29
Tel: 041-5260120
Fax: 041-5261259
A cheaper alternative to those above (L150,000–400,000). Three late 19th-century villas a few minutes from the beach.

TOURIST INFORMATION

The most central tourist office is now the **San Marco APT**, at 71F Piazza San Marco, behind the Museo Correr, tel: 041-529 8711/041-529 8740. This is now the main office for personal callers. (open: 9.30am–5pm or later in summer; until 4.30pm winter). Telephoning the above number puts you in touch with a central switchboard operator who will divert your call to the right information centre in Venice. This is useful since the opening hours of tourist offices in Venice are often subject to change. The other key tourist offices are:
Head office, APT Venice, at Castello 4421 (tel: 041-529 8711; fax: 041-529 8734).
Santa Lucia train station, tel: 041-5298727 (open 8am–7pm; little official documentation but very helpful).
Lido di Venezia (on the island of the Lido), Gran Viale S.M. Elisabetta 6/A; tel: 041-529 8720 (only open from the beginning of May to the end of October; hours variable).
Marco Polo Airport, tel: 041-5415887 (open daily 9.30am–7pm).
Helplines/Advice
Hoteliers freephone number for bookings in Venice (calls from within Italy only): 800-843006
Hoteliers – for last minute booking (from Italy or abroad): 041-5222264
Complaints – on accommodation or other

matters, call the freephone number (in Italy): 800-355 920, and an operator will put you in touch with a department of the local tourist board.
APT Venice website:
www.provincia.venezia.it/aptve

National Call Centre
Italy now provides a new **National Call Centre**, a direct one-stop number for accessing information on events and shows, as well as museums and exhibitions, transport and tourist advice. The operators speak English, French, German and Spanish, as well as Italian, of course. If calling from Italy, it is a freephone number: 800-117700 (open 8am–11pm). However, if calling from abroad, the call is chargeable: 0039-06-419007.

SPECIAL SERVICES

Visitors with Disabilities
Consult the useful *Veneziapertutti* (Venice for all) map which highlights accessible areas and shows that 42 percent of the interesting buildings can be reached without crossing a bridge. The map also lists hotels which are suitable for guests who have a disability. Available from ULSS, Santa Croce 191, free of charge.

Youth Passes
Under 29s are entitled to a Rolling Venice card, which gives discounts on accommodation, restaurants, museums, shops and public transport. The pass costs L6,000 (a useful guidebook and map is an extra L12,000) and is available from all tourist information offices.

Senior Citizens
For the over 60s (on presentation of passport/ID card) entry to the Accademia gallery and Ca' d'Oro is free.

FURTHER READING

Books on Venice and its surroundings are numerous, including many that are out of print. You should be able to find those listed.

Guidebooks and Maps

Insight Guide: Venice, Apa Publications, 1999. Lavishly illustrated and fully revised, with new text, maps and pictures. Includes etailed and informative essays on Venetian culture and history.

Insight Compact Guide: Venice. Apa Publications, 1997. Portable mini-encyclopaedia concentrating on museums, churches and architecture.

Insight Fleximap Venice, Apa Publications, 2000. This hard-wearing laminated fold-out map can be used time and time again.

History

Hibbert, Christopher, *Venice – The Biography of a City,* Grafton Books 1988, reprinted 1992. A superb survey of Venice, which is highly readable and informative; a combination of history, narrative and general guidebook.

Lauritzen, Peter, *Venice – A Thousand Years of Culture and Civilization (the story of Venice)*, Atheneum, New York 1978.

Morris, Jan, *A Sea Voyage*. The voyage concerned is along the historic Venetian trade routes. Jan Morris's text wanders quite effortlessly from past to present. This is a lucid history of the empire, with many interesting insights.

Norwich, John Julius, *A History of Venice*, Penguin 1983. This detailed, well written history up to the end of the republic, is widely regarded as the standard work of Venetian history in English.

Art and Architecture

Liberman, Ralph, *Renaissance Architecture in Venice, 1450–1540*. Frederick Muller Ltd, London, 1982. A detailed account of Venetian architecture from florid late Gothic to High Renaissance.

Ruskin, John, *The Stones of Venice,* 1853. This is *the* classic account of the buildings of Venice, for the serious lover of architecture. The abridged version (edited by J G Links) puts the original work – nearly half a million words – within reach of travellers with limited time.

Steer, John, *Venetian Painting,* Thames & Hudson's 'World of Art' series (UK and US). A well-illustrated and scholarly introduction to the Venetian school.

Novels

Hemingway, Ernest, *Across the River and into the Trees,* Panther 1977 (originally published 1950).

James, Henry, *The Aspern Papers* and *The Wings of the Dove,* Penguin. Evocative accounts from one of the greatest observers of Venice.

Leon, Donna, A series of atmospheric detective novels written about a fictitious Venetian Detective.

Mann, Thomas, *Death in Venice*, Penguin 1971 (originally published in 1921).

Proust, Marcel, *Albertine Disparue* (part of *A la Recherche du Temps Perdu* and translated into English as *The Sweet Cheat Gone* – originally published 1925).

McEwan, Ian, *The Comfort of Strangers* (Picador). Atmospheric chiller, fraught with unease but evocative of the city's melancholic charms.

Others

James, Henry, *Italian Hours*, Century 1988 (originally published 1909). The book includes five essays on Venice in the 1860s and 1870s.

Keates, **Jonathan**, *Italian Journeys* (1991), a sharp memoir with sections on Venice.

McCarthy, Mary, *The Stones of Florence and Venice Observed,* Penguin, 1993, 1956.

Morris, Jan, *Venice*. Faber, revised edition 1993. Brilliantly witty account of the city.

Norwich, John Julius (ed), *Venice, a Travellers' Companion*, Constable, London.

Right: see the city by vaporetto

INSIGHT
Pocket Guides

Insight Pocket Guides pioneered a new approach to guidebooks, introducing the concept of the authors as "local hosts" who would provide readers with personal recommendations, just as they would give honest advice to a friend who came to stay. They also included a full-size pull-out map. Now, to cope with the needs of the 21st century, new editions in this growing series are being given a new look to make them more practical to use, and restaurant and hotel listings have been greatly expanded.

INSIGHT GUIDES

The world's largest collection of visual travel guides

Now in association with

Discovery CHANNEL

Also from Insight Guides...

Insight Guides is the classic series, providing the complete picture with expert and informative text and stunning photography. Each book is an ideal travel planner, a reliable on-the-spot companion – and a superb visual souvenir of a trip. 193 titles.

Insight Maps are designed to complement the guidebooks. They provide full mapping of major destinations, and their laminated finish gives them ease of use and durability. 100 titles.

Insight Compact Guides are handy reference books, modestly priced yet comprehensive. The text, pictures and maps are all cross-referenced, making them ideal books to consult while seeing the sights. 127 titles.

INSIGHT POCKET GUIDE TITLES

Aegean Islands	Canton	Israel	Nepal	Sikkim
Algarve	Cape Town	Istanbul	New Delhi	Singapore
Alsace	Chiang Mai	Jakarta	New Orleans	Southeast England
Amsterdam	Chicago	Jamaica	New York City	Southern Spain
Athens	Corfu	Kathmandu Bikes	New Zealand	Sri Lanka
Atlanta	Corsica	& Hikes	Oslo and Bergen	Stockholm
Bahamas	Costa Blanca	Kenya	Paris	Switzerland
Baja Peninsula	Costa Brava	Kraków	Penang	Sydney
Bali	Costa del Sol	Kuala Lumpur	Perth	Tenerife
Bali Bird Walks	Costa Rica	Lisbon	Phuket	Thailand
Bangkok	Crete	Loire Valley	Prague	Tibet
Barbados	Croatia	London	Provence	Toronto
Barcelona	Denmark	Los Angeles	Puerto Rico	Tunisia
Bavaria	Dubai	Macau	Quebec	Turkish Coast
Beijing	Fiji Islands	Madrid	Rhodes	Tuscany
Berlin	Florence	Malacca	Rome	Venice
Bermuda	Florida	Maldives	Sabah	Vienna
Bhutan	Florida Keys	Mallorca	St. Petersburg	Vietnam
Boston	French Riviera	Malta	San Diego	Yogjakarta
Brisbane & the	(Côte d'Azur)	Manila	San Francisco	Yucatán Peninsula
Gold Coast	Gran Canaria	Melbourne	Sarawak	
British Columbia	Hawaii	Mexico City	Sardinia	
Brittany	Hong Kong	Miami	Scotland	
Brussels	Hungary	Montreal	Seville, Cordoba &	
Budapest	Ibiza	Morocco	Granada	
California,	Ireland	Moscow	Seychelles	
Northern	Ireland's Southwest	Munich	Sicily	

INDEX